Ano Agnivore in a Different Kitchen

Books by Pat Anderson

NOVELS
The McGlinchy Code
The Crimes of Miss Jane Goldie
Torrent
A Toast to Charlie Hanrahan
Catalyst

FACTUAL
Clash of the Agnivores
Fear and Smear
Never Mind the Zombies
Yellow Peril
Rattus Agnivoricus
Damned Agnivores
Up to Our Knees
Get Over It
Another Agnivore in a Different Kitchen

FOR CHILDREN
The Skyscraper Rocket Ship
The Ceremony at Goreb Ridge
The Brain Thing
The Football Star
Mighty Pete and the
School Bully School

Another Agnivore in a Different Kitchen

THE S**T HITS THE FAN

Pat Anderson

Snowy Publications MMXVIII

ISBN: 172048306X
ISBN-13: 978-1720483069

To all the Bampots Utd. Gang.
And to Mick, wherever you are.

Contents

<u>Preface</u>

Well, we've arrived at book number 5 in the series. Who'd have thought when I wrote *Clash of the Agnivores* in 2014 that Neo-Gers would still be around four years later? All the money worries, court cases, changes of personnel etc. would have killed off many a new club. Fortunately for Neo-Gers, their guardian angels at Hampden are always there to look after them.

The way they keep surviving in face of all the odds makes me think that they might outlive us all. I can just see me on my deathbed, dictating the latest volume in the Neo-Gers saga to my nurse. Hopefully not. Surely they can't keep limping on forever!

As I usually do, I'd like to thank Mick, even though it looks as if he's no longer with us. I'd never have got any books sold if he hadn't directed folk toward my blog. His own blog, *Bampots Utd*, is sadly missed.

One group of folk that I've never thanked before, but should have done, is those unsung heroes on Twitter, who re-tweet and post screen-grabs of various funny, interesting and informative pieces. We bloggers rely on them a lot and many of them can be encountered in the end-notes to this book. Thanks again.

I think it's worth repeating the tip I gave in the last book about my online references. Some papers, especially the Daily Record, demand that you complete a survey before viewing an article. Simply click on 'Show me another question' and it invariably takes you straight to the article without having to waste your valuable time. Sometimes they *do* show another question, but another click in the same place soon gets rid of it.

It seems like only yesterday that Boxy arrived at Ibrox with The People and the agnivores praising him to the heavens and talking about all the big-name players he was going to bring in and how he was going to win everything going. The same thing's happening this year and it's hard to see how it's going to end any differently. My great-great-grandchildren will reach '55' long before Neo-Gers do!

Follow me on Twitter: @PatAndrsptr

Follow my blog at: https://paddyontherailway.wordpress.com

Pat Anderson
June 2018

Introduction
Friends of Mine

My last Neo-Gers book was, as usual, published later than I had intended, and the new season had already started by that time. It's worthwhile, though, having a recap, if only to compare the summer of 2017 with that of 2018. It's quite laughable to see how the hopes and expectations were exactly the same and, more than likely, it would all end in exactly the same way.

Boxy's first signing came at the end of May in the shape of Bruno Alves. Who can forget Alves's arrogant assertions about what he was going to do in Scotland?

> I have this feeling and this desire to win and I think to move here will bring this back to me and to my career.
> At almost all the clubs I have played for I win, and I expect to win here for the fans and for the club; I think I can do this here.[1]

And as to why Alves had opted to join Neo-Gers, he was unequivocal.

> I know him (Boxy) and I know about the work he did in Portugal and also some players that he coached before.
> This kind of person can bring a lot to the club and can make the difference. I think Caixinha has the right mentality to bring back the victories and all that everybody wants.[2]

Fandabidosio Cardosio felt the same way about Boxy. 'I like him and what he had to say and he is the right person to put Rangers where it belongs, which is first place.'[3] Daniel Candeias had something similar to say, 'Pedro called me and explained everything about the club and the project. Knowing him and hearing what he told me I would have never been able to say no to this project.'[4]

If the agnivores had thought of it, they'd have called it the 'Caixinha Effect'. It took them another year, however, to come up with a phrase like that. They certainly made a big deal about what a draw Boxy was; it seemed that players were falling over themselves to join his club, even though, like Warbs, he was mostly signing men he already knew. If there's one thing you can say about the agnivores it's that they never change. Mind you, they can't; not if they're properly following Jabba's lead they can't.

Phil Mac Giolla Bhain said, 'Now with the season over The People are now in their happy phase. This will be the case until football matches have to be played again.'[5] Phil was speaking about the end of the season in 2018, but it would equally apply to 2017. In fact, it could easily apply to 2016 as well.

Boxy might have started before the end of the 2016-17 season, but nothing was expected of him in that period. Now, though, he was going to bring in his own players and things were going to be done his way. All the talk was of warchests, going for 55 and all the rest of the clichés we've come to expect from The People and the agnivores. Neo-Gers social media were full of folk that 'couldn't wait' for the new season to come. Celtic weren't going to know what hit them.

After three friendlies in June, in which Boxy's new players hardly figured, it was time for Neo-Gers' first ever foray into European football. Having finished third in the Premiership, Neo-Gers had to start right at the beginning, in the first-round qualifiers for the Europa League. They were hardly going to meet any big names at this level and so it turned out. Their first opponent was a team that nobody had ever heard of: Progres Neiderkorn. This mob had finished fourth in the Luxembourg league, which hardly made them seem like world-beaters.

Progres didn't exactly have a great European pedigree, having only ever played twice in Europe in their ninety-eight-year history and had only scored one goal. They were hardly up there with the big boys, like Barcelona. Then again, they had more of a European history than Neo-Gers.

In the first leg, at Ibrox, five of Boxy's new men played; three of them coming on as substitutes.[6] There was only one goal, however, and it was scored by one of the old guard at Neo-Gers, Kreosote Kenny. 1-0 was hardly a convincing win but, then, maybe the Neo-Gers players were a bit rusty after a month of only taking part in friendlies. They'd do better over in Luxembourg, though; wouldn't they?

As we all know, they didn't; they did worse, being beaten 2-0 on the night and 2-1 on aggregate. They were out of Europe practically before they'd even started. The laughter rang round the world and everyone competed to see who could come up with the best line on Twitter. Gary Lineker said,

> Rangers (sic) lost to a club in Luxembourg. Not Luxembourg but a club in Luxembourg. Not the best team in Luxembourg, the 4th best in Luxembourg.[7]

Paddy Power, meanwhile, chipped in with,

> This is the most embarrassing night for Rangers football club since they stopped being Rangers football club.[8]

We were then treated to the unedifying spectacles of Boxy standing in a bush, arguing with Neo-Gers supporters[9] and The People attacking their own team's bus.[10] Apparently, the word 'Fenian' was bandied about quite a bit that night. The People wanted Boxy out and the season proper hadn't even started yet.

The Daily Record made a desperate attempt to put the result in some kind of context, as if it wasn't as bad as all that.[11] The truth was, however, that Progres Niederkorn was the equivalent of a pub team that nobody had ever heard of. There was no hiding the shame and embarrassment in among other bad results. Comparing it to Celtic's 1-0 loss to Lincoln Red Imps was ridiculous in the extreme; Celtic weren't knocked out of the competition on that occasion.

Boxy's team spent the rest of July playing friendlies, losing only one of them against St. Johnstone. The first game of the new league season started on the 6th August; an away match against Motherwell. It was a close game and one that Neo-Gers only managed to win courtesy of a penalty, awarded by Brother Boaby Madden. Needless to say, Motherwell had a shout for a penalty turned down.[12] It looked like Neo-Gers were going to be as poor as last season and would rely on dodgy decisions to win games.

Incredibly, it was The People that were raging with the referee after their next game. This was against Hibs, whom Neo-Gers still hadn't forgiven for their supporters 'attacking their players' in that Scottish Cup final in 2016. To add to the occasion's piquancy, the Hibs manager was now Neil Lennon, a figure that The People absolutely loathe.

As usual, Lennon was subjected to all manner of abuse, mostly concentrating on his religion and nationality but with the odd shout of 'Paedo' thrown in for good measure. When Hibs went ahead, Lennon made a rather ambiguous gesture with his arm. Of course, The People were incensed and spewed out their fake outrage all over the internet. Hibs won the match 3-2, which made The People even more angry.

During the match, some of the players squared up to one another and it looked as if Ryan Jack had tried to stick the head on Anthony Stokes. The referee had no option but to send him off.[13] Neo-Gers, however, saw things differently and, almost immediately, appealed the red card.[14] That, though, wasn't enough for The People.

With a cheek deserving of a better cause, a supporters' group, calling itself *Follow We Will*, started a petition on Change.org to, as it claimed, 'End The Anti-Rangers (sic) Views Amongst Referees In Scotland!'[15] Just over seven-and-a-half-thousand folk signed this petition, many of them leaving comments. A lot of the comments, however, were made by Celtic supporters taking the mickey out of the whole proceeding.

The season had only just started, and The People were already riled. How much more angry would they get? Well, it was early days and there was a whole season to get through. Despite the calls for him to be sacked after the Progres Niederkorn match, Boxy was still in charge of the Neo-Gers team. When Boxy was around, fun and laughter could never be far away.

Another Agnivore
in a
Different Kitchen

BYE BYE BOXY!

1
Time's Up

After that game against Hibs, when all the church-going innocents among the Ibrox crowd were shocked to their very core by the 'antics' of Neil Lennon, the only word to describe the performance of Neo-Gers was inconsistent. Just like Rangers in May 2011, Neo-Gers were trying for 'three-in-a-row'. Unlike in 2011, however, it had nothing to do with titles; Boxy's team was desperately attempting to win three *matches* in a row, without much success.

In fact, Neo-Gers hadn't managed to win three games in a row since Christmas 2016[1], so it was hard to pin all the blame solely on Boxy. Something, however, was seriously wrong and Boxy was the most obvious scapegoat, as far as The People were concerned. The most sickening aspect, though, was that Celtic were doing extremely well, not having lost a game domestically since May 2016. As one of The People was forced to admit,

> Celtic are miles ahead of us and the rest in Scotland, their manager is also miles ahead of what we have and you can toss the 2 before Pedro in also.[2]

All that The People had to look forward to was seeing Celtic fail in Europe, but even that particular treat had been taken away from them. Some of them might cheer at Celtic being beaten 4-3 by Astana, but the first leg had ended in a 5-0 victory for Celtic and they were through to the Champions League proper. And, of course, in the Second Qualifying Round, they had brushed aside Linfield. Besides, The People themselves were still recovering from the shock of *that* result against Progres Niederkorn.

Celtic making it into the group stages of the Champions League for the second year in a row also meant more money for the club; a commodity that seemed to be seriously lacking at Neo-Gers. The People were aware of this financial disparity but there was nothing they could do about it; or was there? One enterprising soul decided to take matters into his own hands with a petition to UEFA. He said:

> Celtic's victory over Astana has created the awful prospect of them getting into the Champions league which will mean another £30M in revenue.
> This will mean other clubs will fall further behind meaning the end of Scottish football as a competitive league
> We, the undersigned, call on UEFA to think of the good of Scottish football as a whole and ban Celtic from the Champions League.[3]

Now, that's what you call desperate! It obviously didn't occur to this character that the official position of Neo-Gers, the Scottish football authorities and the media was, and is, that money makes no difference. Isn't that what Nimmo Smith said – no sporting advantage? The People obviously realised how ridiculous the thing was since only a couple of hundred have signed it.

But, then, this guy wasn't the only crazy Neo-Gers supporter out there. According to Vanguard Bears, the whole reason why Rangers were docked points when they went into administration and were subsequently 'demoted' was to help Celtic. Apparently, HMRC and even the Westminster Government were in on this conspiracy as well.[4] Obviously, when evolution was going on, this mob went down a different route from the rest of humanity. *Homo fuckingus thickius* is the scientific name.

It was evident from The People constantly going on about Celtic that their own team wasn't doing as well as they thought it should. By the middle of September, Neo-Gers had amassed a total of 11 points from 6 games, but both Celtic and Aberdeen were on 13, each with a game in hand.[5] Still, at least they'd made it into the semi-final of the League Cup, albeit with more than a little help from the match officials.[6]

The 23rd of September was the first game against Celtic this season and The People were pretty bullish in the run up. With Boxy's summer signings, they were convinced that they had improved enough to emerge victorious.[7] The agnivores were the same, coming out with the usual pish about how you couldn't predict an 'Old Firm' encounter, even though there was no such thing anymore.

Of course, it was hard to tell if Boxy was confident or not; to be honest, nobody had a clue what the hell he was on about. He mostly went on about not spending enough time with his family and trying to find his wife something to do to make the time pass less slowly. He did not elaborate on this and we still don't know if he found her a toy-boy or signed her up to a macrame class. When he finally got around to talking about the actual game, he had this to say:

> It's one game that counts for three-points. We know if they get the three points the difference will be eight-points, if we draw everything stays like it is and if we win, which we are working in that direction, we move two-points from them.[8]

Well, that was helpful, wasn't it? At least we were all now aware of what the match meant in terms of points. No indication, though, whether Boxy thought his team could actually win or not.

One thing that cheered up The People no end was the result of the Celtic against Paris Saint-Germain game at Celtic Park in the Champions League proper. Celtic were slaughtered 5-0; their worst-ever European result at home. They were certainly not the 'Invincibles' they made themselves out to be. And hadn't Rangers beaten PSG back in the day?[9] And, since The People's club was 'still Rangers' it was obvious who was going to win at Ibrox.

Neo-Gers, however, are no PSG and Celtic won the match quite comfortably with a score of 2-0. Excuses galore were made for Neo-Gers, including them having 'depleted resources' and 'missing two of their starting defenders'.[10] Morelos was denied a penalty too in the match by that well-known Fenian and terrorist sympathiser, Craig Thomson.[11] Of course, when Ross McCrorie stopped Griffith's ball with his outstretched hand, it was reported as the ball 'inadvertently brushing his hand'.[12] The agnivores were obviously hurting.

It was not a great match by any means but, as usual, Boxy was good entertainment value. Mikael Lustig mistimed a challenge on

Josh Windass on the sideline and clipped the Neo-Gers' player's heel. Windass went sliding off the pitch, straight into poor Boxy, who was sent sprawling.[13] And then, at half-time, he tried to square up to Scott Brown, accusing him of throwing an elbow into a Neo-Gers player in an incident that nobody saw.

At the end of the match, Leigh Griffiths approached the Neo-Gers goal with the intention of tying a Celtic scarf to one of the posts, in a ritual that was becoming somewhat of a tradition. A squad of big, burly security men, however, had beaten him to it and stood guard until the teams went inside.

None of this, however, concerned The People one iota; they had bigger fish to fry. During the match, the Union Bears unfurled a banner, saying, 'Three letters emblazoned on our breast', with a half-hearted card display above it, purportedly representing the badge on the Neo-Gers shirts. Imagine their anger and frustration when the Celtic supporters held up their own banner, with 'Three letters emblazoned on your grave – RIP' on it.[14] The People were absolutely fuming.

Some of them blamed the board, who they accused of letting the Celtic supporters bring in the banner.[15] Others, though, were determined to know who had leaked what was going to be on The People's banner. Somebody called Lloyd Cross got the blame and received all manner of abuse on Twitter. He didn't take this lying down and challenged all and sundry to a 'square go'.[16] The whole thing, though, petered out pretty quickly.

The agnivores, meanwhile, were rather more shaken by what Peter Lawwell was up to. To their utter horror, Lawwell had demanded that the SFA commission an independent review of Rangers' use of EBTs.[17] This was in the wake of the Supreme Court finding in favour of HMRC in July,[18] which cast a different light on Rangers' cheating than the results of the Nimmo-Smith inquiry. In any other country, or sphere of business, this final judgment would have automatically sparked a new enquiry. This, however, was Scotland.

The Scottish media are always filled with stories and opinion-pieces saying how useless the SFA is and how it isn't fit to run a bath, never mind Scottish football. It's okay for them to say so, but not for anyone connected with Celtic. Keith Jackson was quick with the veiled threats, saying that going after those tainted titles would 'open up wounds which will never heal over and also force his club's relationship with Rangers into a whole new world of bitterness and hostility.'[19] He also dredged up all the old shite about how Rangers (sic) had been punished enough.

The Daily Record published an interview with SFA Chief Executive, Stewart Regan, to explain why they weren't complying with Peter Lawwell's request. It was clear which side the Record was on as the article said how Regan 'stood strong', 'was confident and assured' and 'dismissed the conspiracy theorist'.[20] Gary Ralston, the agnivore responsible for the piece, claimed that it was 'a no-holds barred interview' but, really, it was just an attack on Celtic.

Regan claimed that, 'Other than one, we haven't had a single member asking for this (a review) to be undertaken.' It didn't take a genius to work out who that 'one' was but, bearing in mind the IQ of most of his readership, Ralston explained that it meant that 'there's no appetite for a review from any other club than Celtic.'[21] Essentially, it was being made out that Lawwell's request for a review was nothing more than Celtic trying to 'steal' Rangers' titles.

Stephen McIlkenny, in the Scotsman, countered this way of looking at things, saying that Peter Lawwell's words were being twisted:

> Contrary to what some have reported, Celtic are not calling for a review of Rangers, but a review of the governing body as a whole in the light of new evidence. The Parkhead club's statement read: "This is exactly the same position as adopted by the SPFL board on behalf of all Scotland's 42 professional clubs. The club believes that such a review is essential if a line is to be drawn under this whole affair. On that basis, Scottish football could learn lessons and move on."[22]

No doubt McIlkenny's argument would be discounted simply because of his name; it sounds a bit, you know, *Irish*, doesn't it? Meanwhile, those that *do* believe in those conspiracies that Regan had been banging on about were handed a bone, so to speak, when SPFL Chief Executive, Neil Doncaster, wrote to Stewart Regan on behalf of the SPFL Board.

The letter contained the details of what the SPFL Board wanted an enquiry for: to have processes in place to deal with any future financial meltdowns in Scottish football. It was stressed that such a review was not intended to focus on what happened at Rangers. The title of Doncaster's letter, however, suggested otherwise: *Independent review of use of tax avoidance schemes at Rangers FC and actions of Scottish football authorities*.[23] That, surely, could not have been coincidental or unintended.

This immediately left the field open for a letter to the SFA from Neo-Gers, expressing their anger at how Doncaster's missive had been worded. Part of their complaint was over 'why "certain individuals" had so much influence over how the game is being run in Scotland'.[24] Strangely, nobody mentioned anything about 'conspiracy theories' in connection with this Neo-Gers letter. Apparently, they were all ready to accept what The People had been saying for years: that Peter Lawwell runs Scottish football.

Back to matters on the pitch and, before the match against Celtic at Ibrox, the draw was made for the semi-finals of the League Cup, or Betfred Cup as it's become known. Neo-Gers were going to be facing Motherwell, while Celtic would be up against Hibs. Despite the fact that both Motherwell and Hibs were currently playing well, the agnivores were already saying things like, 'Rangers (sic) and Celtic are on course to meet in the final of the Betfred Cup at Hampden'.[25] They were so desperate for Boxy's team to get at least one trophy this season that their hearts were ruling their heads.

Neo-Gers were still in with a chance in all three Scottish competitions. They *could* win the League Cup, they *could* win the Scottish Cup and they *could* even win the league. But, as Kirsty MacColl pointed out in *Fairytale of New York*, so could anyone. It was still early days in the season, and nobody could predict what might happen.

Before the formality of that semi-final against Motherwell, however, Neo-Gers had to bounce back from that defeat against Celtic and knuckle down for their next two league games, which were both away matches against Hamilton and St Johnstone.

They won the match against Hamilton 4-1, despite losing the opening goal, having Ryan Jack sent off and Hamilton being awarded a penalty. Boxy wasn't his usual, animated self on the sidelines, which he put down to his being ill. Being Boxy, though, he couldn't just say that he had the lurgy; he had to wax lyrical. 'I have a fever, I'm sick, I am not well. Sometimes I'm a warrior but the warrior is sometimes sick'.[26] The man's seriously bonkers.

The St Johnstone game was like a Rangers match of old, with the referee ready to give a wee helping hand. Neo-Gers went into the second half holding onto a slender lead of one goal to nil. Saints were putting up a serious fight and the match could have gone either way; until, that is, the Saints captain, Steven Anderson, was sent off in the 71st minute, for tugging somebody's jersey, would you believe.[27] This opened things up for Neo-Gers to bang in two more goals before the final whistle. No doubt, if they hadn't managed to score there would have been a penalty forthcoming.

Despite the agnivores gushing over Carlos Peña,[28] who had managed to keep himself sober enough to play, they were also more than a bit worried. Where was Kreosote Kenny? Why wasn't he playing? Boxy made excuses about him being injured,[29] but nobody was entirely convinced. What the hell was going on?

It's always been evident that the agnivores read Phil Mac Giolla Bhain's blog since bits and pieces always end up in the papers, sometimes being claimed as 'exclusives'. They tend, however, to pick and choose which bits to use or profess to have 'discovered'; they need to stay on the Level with Jabba, after all. They obviously knew fine well what was going on with Kreosote Kenny; it's just that they were reluctant to say.

For weeks, Phil had been telling everyone about the schism at Neo-Gers.[30] Boxy and his team of foreign journeymen were on one side, while the British contingent was on the other. This latter side had its own leader, one whom Phil called the 'Moderator' of the 'Quintessentially British Whatsapp group'.[31] Phil never mentioned this character by name but dropped enough hints for there to be no doubt as to his identity. Suffice it to say that his brown brogues matched his complexion.

This feud appeared to be getting worse as time went on[32] and, with things coming to a head, the powers-that-be at Ibrox were going to have to make a decision. Would they choose Boxy or would they choose KK? Obviously, the feelings of The People would have to be taken into consideration. As far as they were concerned, Boxy had already more than blotted his copybook with the farce in Luxembourg. But, then, unless they read Phil Mac Giolla Bhain's blog, they'd think that everything in the Ibrox garden was rosy. Any move to get rid of anybody would come as a shock. Besides, with Neo-Gers' proclivity for signing folk up on long contracts, could they afford to get rid of anybody?

The Ibrox board could content itself that it didn't have to deal with such things just yet. There was a long way to go in the season, so it had plenty of time, didn't it? Things, however, didn't exactly turn out the way the board had hoped. It wasn't only The People that were reaching the end of their tether; Honest Dave was too.

If the agnivores were confident that the semi-final match against Motherwell was a formality, Boxy appeared even more confident. At least it seemed that way; it wasn't easy to tell. Instead of caravans, dogs and families, this time he was going on about vampires. Yes, you did read that correctly; vampires! He said,

> The vampires taste the flavour of the blood and they want more, they need it.
> It's the same with the competitive teams and clubs, competitive players and competitive managers. They like the way the blood tastes.[33]

Well, he certainly had bats in his belfry! Gordon Waddell, in the Sunday Mail used the euphemism 'colourful' to describe him, which was like calling Hitler 'a bit naughty'. Boxy went on to explain his metaphor:

> I did it at Santos Laguna in Mexico and it's like a sort of addiction, you know?
> People are addicted to smoking or eating good or playing sport. I am an addict to the win – that's why I work so hard because my focus is to win.[34]

He must have been suffering serious DTs at Neo-Gers, then. He also disparaged Motherwell's players; or, at least, he seemed to, going on about how, 'they play good football, but it is their way. They play good football their way' and 'if you put these players in another place ask them to perform another game ... that's another question'.[35] What the hell was all that about? We could only assume, as Waddell seemed to, that he thought he was going to win.

14

When it came to Motherwell's physicality, Boxy had more insane ramblings to proffer, arguing that his team didn't need to use the same tactics.

> No, I'm not that type of guy. In the time of the cowboys, we used to say, 'eye by eye and teeth by teeth', but now they have found the weapons, it is not like that anymore…More than energy, we require cleverness.[36]

What they really required was having the referee on their side, as usual. As for cleverness, that has never been an attribute in abundance at Ibrox, whether at the old team or the new. Rangers, moreover, had been a by-word for thuggery and the new team had the same reputation. Still, pretending that Neo-Gers was a clever, skillful team was the least of the lies about the new club.

The match itself was full of talking points, with both managers being sent to the stands. Neo-Gers were convinced that they'd been kicked all over the pitch and Keith Jackson agreed, going on about the 'treatment dished out to' Morelos.[37] Anyone would think they'd lost the match. In fact, they did, being beaten 2-0. It wasn't like Neo-Gers to be bad losers, was it?

The thing that got Neo-Gers riled up the most was Fandabidosio Cardosio being elbowed in the face. Bruno Alves felt that this epitomised the whole match, with Motherwell getting away with murder. He said,

> I don't like to find excuses for when we lose but for me it is really disappointing. You start off playing football and then you are playing other things.
> I am sad because we lost the game and I am sad about what happened. Fabio broke his nose. I am disappointed with this.[38]

He was disappointed, then. His disappointment, though, was as nothing compared to that of the Neo-Gers high command when they found out that Alves himself was the only one cited in the Compliance Officer's report. Alves had kicked out at another player while he, Alves, was on the ground, which, in anybody's book, is a red-card offence. The word from Ibrox somewhat betrayed the feelings there: 'Rangers (sic) are not seeking to make excuses for losing the match.'[39] Aye, right!

The player being demonised in the press for breaking Cardosio's nose was Ryan Bowman. Anyone that saw the match could tell, and you can also tell from the picture in the Daily Record,[40] that he didn't mean to do it and he certainly didn't have much room to manoeuvre with Cardosio's arms wrapped round him.

The Neo-Gers website puts an entirely different spin on things. It says, 'Fabio Cardoso had to be replaced by Ross McCrorie on 66 minutes after he was caught by *Louis Moult* and had blood pouring from his nose.'[41] (My italics) Now, that little mistake was calculated to get the blood of The People boiling, since Moult not only scored the first goal, but the second, which put the game beyond Boxy's team. Were Neo-Gers suggesting that Moult shouldn't have been on the pitch to score that second goal? What was that they were saying about 'not seeking to make excuses for losing'?

Boxy himself had plenty to say but, as usual, nobody had a clue what he was on about:

> How many transfer windows did we have so far? How many months are we in the club? How many more things do we need to change? How many years have Rangers been out of the Scottish system?
> Are we happy with the direction Scottish football is going? How many international referees are in the last stages of the biggest competitions? How many Scottish players are known European-wide? How long has the UEFA co-efficient been going down? How long has the national team been absent from the biggest competitions?[42]

The only possible thing to take from all that was that it wasn't Boxy's fault that his team had lost; it was everybody else's. Even the agnivores were flummoxed, one of them asking, 'What has this got to do with losing to Motherwell?'[43] He was told, 'Everything. You have the connection.'[44] Eh?

The People were a lot clearer than Boxy about things; they wanted him out.

16

Caixinha is an embarrassment to my club and he should have driven straight to the airport from Hampden. His touchline antics were cringeworthy and he's built a side with no heart. Motherwell beat us because they had the passion and spirit which cost the club next to nothing.[45]

The same Daily Record page had a survey, in which 60% wanted rid of Boxy. Incongruously, the Record also had a slideshow of pictures with the title, 'Can You Spot Yourself in the Crowd?' Would the Neo-Gers supporters recognise themselves from the backs of their heads as they tried to sneak out of Hampden?

The agnivores were just as angry as The People, with Keith Jackson opining that Boxy's failures were reflecting badly on Honest Dave King. He felt, like The People, that Boxy should be sacked and that if King didn't act soon, then his own reputation as a 'saviour' was at risk. You had to laugh, though, at the way Jackson described Boxy, saying he 'has been so hopelessly out of his depth since he was first plucked from the obscurity of a Qatari desert by King's three wise men.'[46]

Dearie me, that's not what Jackson and his paper were saying about Boxy when he first arrived at Ibrox. It had only been seven months since they were going on about action men, bullfighting and speedboats. Back then, he'd been the greatest thing since Warburton sliced bread and nobody seemed able to talk about him without mentioning Mourinho in the same breath. What a difference half a year makes!

Unfortunately for Boxy, Honest Dave had made the trip from South Africa to see his team book its place in the League Cup final. He certainly wouldn't have been a happy bunny. Seated next to him was Kreosote Kenny, left out of Boxy's team yet again.[47] No doubt he had to make excuses, so he could go off and piss himself laughing in the executive bogs.

Honest Dave was still in Glasgow on the Wednesday and made one of his rare appearances at Ibrox to see Neo-Gers play Kilmarnock. Sharing the Director's Box with him was Boxy, banned from the touchline for his tantrum at Hampden.[48] Both of them had to sit and suffer a 1-1 draw, with Candeias missing a penalty, Ryan Jack being sent off (yet again) and Kilmarnock scoring in the 95th minute.[49] It was a sore one to take. Boxy spoke after the match, offering his apologies to The People.

> I say to them that they are the most loyal fans in the world.
> They don't deserve to pass through this situation.
> As I've told you all the time we work for them and I'm more disappointed for them.
> Because besides being the Rangers manager I'm also a Rangers fan. I'm blue inside.[50]

Nobody, however, was interested. The People had been making their feelings plain for some time and the agnivores were joining in as well.[51] And that wasn't all; the board decided to call an emergency meeting the day after the Kilmarnock game.[52] It looked as if Boxy's reign of error was coming to an end.

Sure enough, at a quarter to three, the news was posted on the Daily Record web page: Boxy had been told to take his dogs, his camels, his vampire bats and his whole menagerie and bugger off.[53] He had only lasted 229 days; apparently only beaten by Paul Le Guen for the record of the shortest-serving manager, of either club, at Ibrox[54] Actually, details of the start of Le Guen's tenure are pretty thin on the ground; all anyone says is that he began the job in the summer of 2006. His first signing, though, was Dean Furman, who put pen to paper on the 10th May.[55] Even going from that date, Le Guen was in charge for 241 days – a good twelve days longer than Boxy. Boxy is, then, the shortest-serving manager ever at Ibrox. Le Guen's record of being the shortest-serving manager at Rangers, however, is secure; Rangers died in 2012.

The joy of The People and the agnivores at Boxy's departure wasn't shared by the rest of us. We were going to seriously miss his lunatic ramblings. Boxy himself, meanwhile, went back to Mexico to take charge of Cruz Azul. The last we heard of him, he was getting bottles thrown at him by his own team's supporters.[56] It'll take a lot more than that to get our Boxy down, though!

2
Something's Gone Wrong Again

Once Boxy was out the door, it was time for Martin Luther lookalike Graeme Murty to step into the breach once more. Everybody remembered him for that 1-1 draw at Celtic Park,[1] before Boxy came along and spoiled the party. The obvious conclusion was that he would do a better job than Boxy. Yet again, though, his appointment was only an interim one; the search for a new manager was on.

The media were quick to come up with suitable replacements for Boxy, suggesting Mikel Arteta, Frank De Boer, Tommy Wright, Alex McLeish, Patrick Vieira, Chris Coleman, Billy Davies and even Sam Allardyce.[2] How Neo-Gers would be able to afford some of those names nobody explained. The bookies' favourite for the job, though, was Derek McInnes. There was a slight problem there; McInnes had a contract with Aberdeen until 2020. If Neo-Gers wanted him, then they'd have to pay for him.

It was only a few days later that Aberdeen set the price that Neo-Gers would have to pay: £1.5m.[3] So confident were The People that McInnes would soon be coming to Ibrox that one of them felt able to comment, 'Welcome to Rangers Derek. Scotland's biggest and most successful club.'[4] The fact that Neo-Gers hadn't even spoken to McInnes yet was the least that was wrong with that statement!

While it might be doubtful that Neo-Gers had that kind of money to pony up in one lump sum, it seemed that they didn't mind adding to the monthly payroll. On the 30th October it was announced that Mark Allen, the Neo-Gers Director of Football, had appointed Andy Scoulding as Chief Scout and promoted academy scout, Billy McLaren as his assistant. At the same time, Dave Swanick was appointed Allen's 'man on the Continent', while, inexplicably, Swanick's counterpart in Britain was Bomber Brown! Allen said of Brown,

> When you go back and look at some of those characteristics I mentioned in terms of the player profile, John is well-known to have had that history with Rangers Football Club and will know what a Rangers (sic) player looks like. He will be able to identify those sorts of characteristics.[5]

Presumably, that meant Brown knew about things like players having gone to the 'right' school and being conversant with funny handshakes. The appointment would also keep The People happy; another Real Raynjurz Man never went amiss. Oh, and Katy Lamont was made Player Liaison Officer,[6] whatever the hell that is.

As the days turned to weeks, things hadn't moved on the manager front and it appeared that no approach at all had been made to either Aberdeen or McInnes. The natives started to get restless. Both Barry Ferguson and Kris Boyd expressed concern at the apparent lack of movement and Ferguson felt frustrated and disappointed. 'I'm frustrated, disappointed,' he said.[7] He also had this to say about any appointee: 'I think it's got to be somebody who knows the club, who knows the traditions and the expectations at Rangers.'[8] No more Catholics, then.

At the AGM, King explained how the club had to take its time to find the right person, saying that 'sometimes it takes three months for him to hire executives in South Africa.'[9] He also hinted that the preferred candidate was under contract, increasing the expectation that McInnes was their man. The People seemed happy enough with his story at any rate. But why was it taking so long?

Honest Dave's interview with Rangers (sic) TV after the AGM gave a clue. He said,

> You've got to talk to clubs and talk about compensation. It has taken longer than we would have maybe liked, but not longer than is necessary.[10]

Now, that sounded as if Neo-Gers were haggling over how much compensation they needed to pay. Aberdeen had set the amount at

20

£1.5m and if Neo-Gers were determined to get their man as soon as possible, then they would have just handed over the cash. The fact it was taking so long suggested that Neo-Gers simply didn't have the money.

Meanwhile, Graeme Murty was getting on with the job in hand, with varying success. For his first game in charge, Murty brought Kreosote Kenny back in from the cold. It was an away match against Hearts, against whom Neo-Gers could only manage a miserable 0-0 draw at Ibrox back in August. This time, though, KK scored two goals and assisted in another to make the full-time result a 3-1 victory. The media were fulsome in their praise of Murty; he was succeeding where Boxy had failed.[11]

A 3-0 defeat of Partick Thistle at Ibrox followed and then, two weeks later, after the international break, the *Curse of Neo-Gers* struck again. Just like Warbs and Boxy, Murty just couldn't get those elusive three wins in a row. The crowd mostly left Ibrox before full-time as Neo-Gers lost 2-0 to Hamilton.[12] It looked as if McInnes couldn't come quickly enough.

Finally, Neo-Gers made their move, only to be told where to go by Aberdeen chairman, Stewart Milne. Apparently, Neo-Gers offered a million, which Milne immediately turned down. The only option McInnes had, if he wanted to speak to Neo-Gers, was to resign as Aberdeen manager. According to Keith Jackson, this was exactly what McInnes wanted. A 'source' told Jackson that

> By turning down the Rangers (sic) offer he (Milne) has effectively kicked the ball straight into Derek's court. He now faces a difficult decision but if he wants to be the next manager of Rangers (sic) – and it seems very much that he does – then he knows now what he has to do.[13]

Jackson himself opined that McInnes was 'determined to listen to what Rangers (sic) have to say even if that results in a messy divorce from Aberdeen'. In fact, the headline of Jackson's article screamed, 'Derek McInnes to quit Aberdeen for Rangers (sic)'.[14] If the Daily Record sports writer was to be believed, then McInnes was on his way to Ibrox.

Only twenty-four hours after Jackson's article, a statement appeared on the Aberdeen website. The main point of the statement was contained in part of what Stewart Milne had to say:

> Derek appreciates all that he has at this Club and feels he wants to keep driving the Club forward. This is where he

wants to be and he feels he very much has unfinished business with Aberdeen FC.

I personally am delighted that Derek has decided to remain with the Club and everyone looks forward to putting the speculation of the past few weeks behind us and concentrating on matters on the park starting at Dens tomorrow evening.[15]

Neo-Gers were furious to have lost out on their number-one target. After all those weeks of the media going all-out to unsettle McInnes and persuade him that his future lay at Ibrox, the whole pursuit had fallen at the final hurdle. McInnes had said, 'No'. The reaction of the club was characteristically petulant, almost making it seem as if they'd never really wanted McInnes in the first place.

We were subsequently made aware by Aberdeen's statement that, at this stage in his career, it would be best for him to remain in his current post. We endorse that position because moving to a massive club like Rangers is a big step with concomitant risk. We continue to consider candidates but will only appoint someone in whom we have full confidence and who feels he is ready for the job.[16]

So petty, pathetic and completely embarrassing was this statement, even The People felt red-faced. Neo-Gers forums were full of folk condemning it and, at the same time, condemning the board that had produced it.[17] Tom English was of the opinion that this was a serious turning-point for Honest Dave and his board. As he put it:

There comes a time when being better than the Easdale brothers is not enough anymore. The tortured Mark Warburton saga, followed by the expensive catastrophe of Pedro Caixinha, followed by the protracted and failed pursuit of McInnes, has caused significant reputational damage to this Rangers board. This is not outsiders talking. It's their own people.[18]

This shows a remarkable lack of insight on the part of English; The People don't mind criticising their own board, but they hate anyone else doing it. And it's not just that; The People need their 'Real Raynjurz Men' at the top of the marble staircase to help maintain the illusion that the new club is 'still Rangers'. Nothing else matters. Remember, they chased out a real billionaire and replaced him with a crook, just because the latter said he was a Rangers supporter and used to be on the board of the old club. All that concerns The People is that the 'right' sort are in charge at Ibrox and, if Catholics can't be banned completely, then at least they should keep their heads down. Their anger at King wouldn't last very long.

So, why *did* McInnes turn Neo-Gers down? Well, opinion appears to be not just divided on that one, but fragmented. Essentially, though, they all arrive at the same conclusion in the end. Tom English, for example, thought that McInnes wasn't too chuffed about the amount of time it took Neo-Gers to make a move for him. That, combined with concerns he had about how much control he would have at Ibrox made up his mind for him.[19]

Keith Jackson had a different take on Tom English's theory. He said, 'The six-week wait for an official approach to be made to Aberdeen did little to give him confidence that the Rangers regime were truly united in their desire to make him their man.'[20] In this scenario, all the dithering made McInnes feel that there were those in the Ibrox boardroom that didn't want him at Neo-Gers.

Strangely, this didn't sound like Jackson's usual Jabba-fed story; you can say what you like about Traynor, but he never bites the hand that's paying him. Was Jackson making a long-overdue bid for independence? There was certainly a decent argument for saying that Jackson was onto something with his analysis.

According to Phil Mac Giolla Bhain, it's possible that McInnes got wind of the little matter of some of The People, apparently important men, not so much objecting to McInnes but his assistant, Tony Docherty. Phil gave an example of just what that objection was.

> If McInnes is our next manager our board must make
> sure they do not under any circumstances allow that
> anti Rangers bheast supporting cunt tony Docherty

anywhere near our club the sheep can keep him & if McInnes insists he can go tay fuck anaw[21]

As you can see, The People are not too hot when it comes to punctuation. The message, though, is pretty clear. Only one sort of person would take a job with bigots like that; unfortunately for Neo-Gers, McInnes wasn't one of them.

And it wasn't just bigotry that was behind Neo-Gers not wanting Tony Docherty. On the 21st November, the Daily Star ran a story that said that Neo-Gers were insisting that Jonatan Johansson and Graeme Murty remain as part of the first-team staff. Apparently, this was proving a sticking point, not just for McInnes but for any potential manager.[22] Most managers prefer to appoint their own coaching staff, not inherit one from the previous boss. If Neo-Gers were insisting on this condition, then how many others would they put upon a new manager?

Which brings us back to Tom English's opinion that McInnes didn't take the job because he wouldn't have enough control. As we have seen, there were quite a few factors involved but, essentially, English was right; McInnes wasn't going to be able to have his own way at Neo-Gers. Why the hell would he turn the gratitude and adoration of Stewart Milne and the Aberdeen fans into bitterness, for a job in which he couldn't be sure what his remit would be?

Besides, McInnes was no doubt smart enough to realise that, if he went to Ibrox, he'd be a prisoner of the Big Lie. If you've seen the movie *Men In Black*, you'll remember Tommy Lee Jones telling Will Smith, 'A person is smart; people are dumb'. He could well have added. 'The People are even dumber'. Ever since Neo-Gers was born, The People have been desperate to believe the Big Lie; that the club they are supporting is not new at all but is still Rangers. This is a comfort blanket; it is also, however, a curse, especially for any manager of the club.

The belief that Neo-Gers is still Rangers; a belief encouraged by the Scottish media and football authorities, means that the old sense of entitlement is still strong among The People. Blinded to reality by the Big Lie, they simply cannot understand why their team isn't winning everything and sitting on top, where they believe it should be. This means that any manager of that team is on a hiding to nothing.

24

Warbs told them and Boxy told them; it would take time to build a team that could challenge Celtic. Nobody, however, wanted to listen. The People demanded immediate success, the agnivores clamoured for it and the Neo-Gers board desperately tried to provide it. Neither Warbs nor Boxy were up to that particular job and had to go. McInnes probably realised that his tenure would end in exactly the same way.

There was, of course, another side to the McInnes debacle: money. Neo-Gers couldn't afford to pay the appropriate compensation to Aberdeen or to reimburse McInnes if he were to buy out his own contract.[23] The whole business had been a complete waste of time, done simply to con The People and the agnivores into thinking that Neo-Gers had tried their best to find a new manager.

Neo-Gers left it a couple of weeks before announcing who their new manager was. It was hardly a surprise.

> The Club's directors believe Graeme has demonstrated he is capable of handling this task successfully and are confident the players will continue to respond to his leadership in a positive manner. With so much still at stake in the current season this decision was not taken lightly but now that Graeme has been given full control he can work towards the obvious targets with greater focus.[24]

Murty was the cheapest option and, really, all that cash-strapped Neo-Gers could afford. That fact, however, couldn't possibly be imparted to The People; there would have been mass nervous breakdowns. The agnivores, as usual, were there to make sure only good news was imparted. 'The former Scotland international has convinced Ibrox chiefs he is the man to lead Rangers forward'.[25] That made it sound as if, after a lot of deliberation, it had been decided that Murty was the best man for the job. Well, he *was* the best man; the best man they could find in the bargain basement.

Give Murty his due; he had managed to break the curse of the *three-in-a-row* and even succeeded in equalling Neo-Gers' record in the Premiership of *four* wins in a row. Yes, there had been losses, but he certainly didn't appear to be any worse than either Warbs or

Boxy. Two of those wins had been against Aberdeen and one against Hibs, making it look like Neo-Gers were going to be serious contenders for second place. As usual, though, controversy was never far away.

The first game against Aberdeen was at Ibrox and refereed by Andrew Dallas, who made sure Neo-Gers got their customary penalty, while denying one for Aberdeen. He was certainly showing that he was his father's son! He also sent off an Aberdeen player near the end of the match when it looked as if the visitors were mounting a comeback. Remarkably, on the scoresheet was one Carlos Peña; he must have been allowed a hair-of-the-dog in the changing room before kick-off.[26]

Four days later, the two sides met again at Pittodrie. There was no Andrew Dallas there this time so Windass was booked for diving in the box, while it was Neo-Gers turn to play with ten men, Ryan Jack being sent off, yet again, on the 56th minute. The Ibrox club, however, still managed to win 2-1 and it seemed as if all the media speculation over McInnes was having an effect on him and his team.[27]

After a 2-1 home win against Ross County, in which County boss, Owen Coyle, felt his side had been denied a stick-on penalty,[28] it was time to face Neil Lennon's Hibs side again, this time at Easter Road. It was another 2-1 victory for Neo-Gers, although, once again, their opposition was denied a clear penalty for hand-ball.[29]

And so Neo-Gers climbed into second place with a bit of help from the match officials. It was just like the good old days when Rangers played at Ibrox. They only led Aberdeen on goal difference, however, and it wasn't to last.

Rather unfortunately, Murty's last match before his appointment to take charge for the rest of the season had been a 3-1 defeat at home to St Johnstone.[30] And then, just one day after the Neo-Gers announcement, Neo-Gers lost again, this time at Rugby Park. The score was 2-1, with both Kilmarnock's goals being scored by the massive bulk that was Kris Boyd.[31] Things couldn't get more embarrassing. Well, perhaps they could; only a week later, Neo-Gers were due at Celtic Park.

There was, however, a midweek game before the match against Celtic; it was at home against Motherwell. It ended in a 2-0 victory, which gave The People renewed confidence and the agnivores licence to bang on about 'gaps closing' and the like.

The game at Celtic Park was actually quite exciting, even though it ended 0-0.[32] There were a lot of missed chances and Neo-Gers defended better than usual, obviously having been coached by those stewards that had kept Leigh Griffiths away from the Ibrox goalposts back in September.

The People were overjoyed; as was the club, who said, 'Rangers (sic) more-than (sic) earned their draw at Parkhead this afternoon with a superb performance – but it's a game they may look back on wondering "what if" after missing a number of great chances to take the three points back to Ibrox.'[33]

The agnivores, too, were in orgasmic mode, praising Neo-Gers to the hilt. Craig Swan, in the Daily Record, said, 'Rangers will leave Celtic Park a bit disappointed that they didn't claim all three points'.[34] He did concede that 'Celtic were not at their best' but his article was full of how brilliant Neo-Gers had been. Yet again, they were coming down the road.

It is perhaps worth noting that, prior to the Celtic v Neo-Gers match on 30th December, Celtic had played eleven more games than Neo-Gers. And it's not just the games themselves; having to travel around Europe takes its toll and Celtic certainly looked tired against Neo-Gers. A bit of a rest was in order and it was fortunate for Celtic that the winter break was upon us.

There wouldn't be so much R & R for Neo-Gers, though. They were going over to Florida to take part in the prestigious Florida Cup, against the best that the World had to offer. At least, that was the story in the papers.

3
Harmony in My Head

After Neo-Gers' ignominious exit from Europe at the hands of Progres Niederkorn, they were desperate for some 'glamour' friendlies to make themselves appear relevant in European and World football. Thank God they'd been invited to play Benfica in the annual Eusebio Cup. In a break from the usual procedure, where Benfica played at home in a pre-season match against top opposition, the game against Neo-Gers was to take place in October at Tim Hortons Field in Hamilton, Ontario.[1]

It was only a few days before the match was due to take place that the whole thing was cancelled. Neo-Gers often boasts of its 'worldwide' fan base but, it appeared, none of them were buying tickets.[2] For some reason, the organisers, Elite Soccer Entertainment, felt the need to apologise to Neo-Gers for blaming their supporters. They still cited poor ticket sales, though as the reason for cancelling. Now, there are a lot more Scottish immigrants in Ontario than there are Portuguese, so it's pretty obvious which team's fans weren't stumping up.[3]

Instead of this 'glamour' friendly, Neo-Gers ended up playing a 'non-glamour' friendly against Greenock Morton. So unglamorous was this particular game that it was played behind closed doors at Murray Park.[4] (Oops! Sorry. I forgot they're calling it *Auchenhowie* these days.) The game ended in a 3-3 draw,[5] which I don't suppose was the kind of score Boxy wanted. Just as well they weren't playing against Benfica, eh?

It was also just as well that Neo-Gers had another 'glamour' fixture lined up; in fact, more than one 'glamour' fixture. They were going to be participating in the Florida Cup, a tournament taking place, unsurprisingly, in Florida, during the January break. The Daily Record, of course, heralded the tournament in excited tones.

> Pedro Caixinha's side will take part in the glamour tournament Stateside during the Premiership winter break.

And organisers have now revealed Polish side Legia Warsaw and Fluminense of Brazil will join other teams from around the world in an eight-club tourney.[6]

It certainly seemed glamorous and prestigious, if the organisers' Facebook page was to be believed.

Florida Cup is the biggest winter preseason football competition in the world. Top players from Europe and South america (sic) represent their clubs and nations in an international football showdown.[7]

'Top players…'? So why the hell were Neo-Gers invited? The answer might lie in the blurb on the official Florida Cup website. 'Where clubs become nations,' it says. Obviously, that means that a country can bask in the reflected glory of one of their teams winning the tournament. Presumably, the organisers expect a whole nation to get behind the team representing it; which shows what the organisers know about football. But that blurb also, quite probably, has another, more arcane meaning.

Remember that old quiz, *Blockbusters*? There were other quizzes too where schoolchildren took part and even *Open to Question*, where politicians and the like answered questions from teenage school pupils. The one constant in all these programmes was that it was always wee, posh gits that appeared on them. I remember reading one teenager's letter in the Daily Record, asking how he went about applying for one of these shows. The answer was that the programmes' producers always contacted local authorities and asked them to recommend schools. You can just imagine which schools were chosen.

I believe the same kind of situation arose with the Florida Cup. The organisers contacted the SFA, asking them to put forward a team to represent Scotland. It's obvious which team the SFA would select; the team that it had bent over backwards to accommodate for the past five-and-a-bit years and whose predecessor received the same, preferential treatment. It's the only possible explanation as to why Neo-Gers were going to be turning up in Florida.

There were eight teams taking part: Neo-Gers, PSV Eindhoven, Legia Warsaw, Corinthians, Atlético Mineiro, Fluminense, Atlético Nacional and Barcelona (no, not that one, but a team from

Ecuador).[8] Although the organisers were calling it a tournament, all the teams didn't play against each other. It wasn't a knock-out tournament either. It was a weird business where every team only played two games and then buggered off home to wait to see if they'd won the Cup. There were three points for a win, one for a draw and an extra point if you won the resulting penalty shoot-out. The ultimate winner was decided on points, then goal difference, goals for and then goals against; just like a normal tournament.[9]

Presumably, there was a draw made for who was going to play whom and Neo-Gers were paired with Brazilian team Atlético Mineiro on January 11th and then, another Brazilian team, Corinthians, on January 13th.[10] And that would be it. No hanging about. Nobody would know who'd won the thing probably until January 20th, the last day of the tournament.

The lustre was taken off the tournament somewhat when Atlético Mineiro announced that they would be sending their reserve team, which played in Brazil's third tier. They didn't want to risk any of their first-team players picking up injuries. The Atlético Director of Football said: 'We have concluded that preparation for the new season at a training camp is more important than playing in a tournament.'[11] Oh, dear! Suddenly that 'prestigious' tournament didn't look quite so prestigious anymore.

Neo-Gers won their first match against Atlético Mineiro 1-0, which had the club crowing about it on their website. 'Josh Windass' (sic) stunning strike on 68 minutes gave Rangers (sic) a deserved win in their first Florida Cup match at the Orlando City Stadium tonight.'[12] The Daily Record, predictably, joined in the praise.

It was hard not to laugh at the DR saying that Neo-Gers youngster, Serge Atakayi, 'was playing at this level for the first time'.[13] What level? Were they honestly saying that Atakayi had never played against kids his own age before? As for the rest of the team, everyone seemed to be forgetting that they were competing against a bunch of weans from Brazil's third division.

The match against Corinthians ended in a 4-2 victory, with Neo-Gers making a comeback from being 2-0 down at half-time. A 'cracking comeback,' the Daily Record called it, 'after Graeme Murty rang the changes at half-time'.[14] The DR report on the Atlético Mineiro match had spoken of a 'friendly tournament'.[15]

Now, however, with the possibility that Neo-Gers might win the thing, it was simply a 'tournament'.[16]

Since it actually *was* a friendly tournament, there was no restriction on the number of substitutions that could be made. Neo-Gers made seven changes for the second half and were still able to replace Foderingham when he got injured.[17] Corinthians changed practically the whole team as well after half-time and that was probably what cost them the match. Like Atlético Mineiro, they no doubt wanted to avoid any of their main players being injured.

The Daily Record excitedly showed Neo-Gers at the top of the competition table, but things weren't over yet. Yes, there were four teams that no longer had a chance, but the other three teams hadn't even kicked a ball in anger yet.[18] Still, as the squad made its way home, it couldn't be denied that Neo-Gers were in with a shout. The People and the agnivores held their breath in anticipation.

Not only did Neo-Gers have a chance of winning the tournament, the way the agnivores banged on about one of their players there was the possibility that he might win the trophy presented to the best player in the competition. 'Alfredo Morelos inspires stunning fightback to give Ibrox men chance of Florida Cup success' screamed the headline about the win over Corinthians.[19] This was only the start of the attempt to make Morelos seem like a world-class player, but more about that later.

There are certainly bragging rights involved if you're named Player of the Tournament in any competition, but being selected as such in the Florida Cup is probably something you wouldn't want to put on your C.V. The problem is that this particular accolade is sponsored by Disney World and is called, believe it or not, the 'Mickey Mouse Trophy'![20] The trophy itself is actually a statuette of the famous rodent. Imagine that sitting on your mantelpiece!

I can't discover anywhere who it was that won the coveted trophy this year. The winner's probably asked for anonymity; too embarrassed to let anybody know. For all we know, Morelos *did* win it and Mickey is safely ensconced in the Ibrox Trophy Room, next to the Petrofac Cup.

Deep down, everyone connected with Neo-Gers knew that the Florida Cup was a pretty meaningless competition. The Neo-Gers website spoke of it being 'an excellent workout',[21] while the Daily Record said, after the Atlético Mineiro game, that 'it was only a Florida

Cup friendly on their winter break'.[22] That, however, did not stop the agnivores from posting live updates on the two matches, as well as endless analyses.[23] You could have been forgiven for thinking Neo-Gers were in the latter stages of the Champions League.

The People, too, were overexcited and followed the final games closely.[24] Unfortunately for them, Neo-Gers ended up coming third. Atlético Nacional won the competition, with Barcelona SC runners-up. Fortunately for the rest of us, Neo-Gers ended up coming third. If they had won, we'd never have heard the end of it.

Of course, The People can't go anywhere without bringing themselves, their team and their country into disrepute; just ask the people of Manchester and Barcelona. This time there were no riots and there was no fighting (that we know of) but there was the usual, rousing chorus of *The Billy Boys*. Unfortunately, this made it onto the official, Florida Cup promotional video on YouTube.[25]

Condemnation was quick and even the anodyne *Nil By Mouth* joined in, saying,

> It's sad when groups of fans tarnish their club's reputation abroad by packing bigotry in the suitcase and then putting it on display at matches.
> These people need to join the 21st century rather than living in the dark ages.[26]

That was an uncharacteristically explicit and direct comment from NBM. Normally, their main concern is to maintain 'balance' and it was surprising that Celtic supporters weren't drawn into their condemnation. Maybe if they were this open and direct more often they might actually do something about bigotry in Scotland.

Anyway, the organisers of the Florida Cup were extremely embarrassed and apologetic; they weren't to know what the song was about. TV presenter Fabio Brazza was mortified when he discovered what he'd been dancing around to on the video. He'd asked the Neo-Gers supporters to teach him a song or a chant and he had tried to join in, thinking he was learning a *football* song. He said,

> I feel very sad and betrayed that it happened, and that my image, and Florida Cup's image is in it.

The purpose of the tournament is totally the opposite of the chanting. Our goal is to promote a great experience for all family and bring people from different culture's together.

On my behalf and in Florida Cup's name I am really sorry to what happened.[27]

The blonde in the video,[28] Alicia Wiggins, had a typical, Neo-Gers supporter reaction when questioned about the incident. She said, 'It wasn't just me'.[29] Well, that made everything alright, then.

The People were unrepentant about the whole thing, not seeing anything wrong with either *The Billy Boys* or the other song heard in the video with the words, *We hate Celtic – Fenian bastards*. As usual, they lashed out at others.

Not illegal in Florida so fûck them.[30]

I must have missed their report about the Tim fans singing sectarian songs when they were getting thrashed in Europe.[31]

What about the 150 tarrier attacking a pub has that had a mention in the msn?[32]

Freedom of speech is still a thing in America so feck them.[33]

Why have they (Celtic fans) been in touch with the sponsors of the Florida cup and grassing to the rags about that lassie singing the Billy boys???[34]

And that was that. It's doubtful that Neo-Gers will ever be invited back to the Florida Cup after embarrassing the organisers the way they did. The People, however, never see things as they really are and will look to blame everybody else. The organisers of the tournament will be blamed for being too sensitive and too PC. The People's ire will also be directed at the SFA, the Scottish media and, of course, Celtic and its supporters. They're nothing if not predictable.

Predictable too was how the Daily Record summed up the trip in an interview with Neo-Gers player, David Bates. Young Master Bates felt that it had been a great bonding exercise, which would set the team up for the remainder of the season. They went to an ice-hockey match and to Universal Studios and got hot-dogs and ice-cream and candy-floss and candy apples and…and…and…everything! David slept well that night!

Laughably, the Record chipped in with how it had been a 'hard graft' against 'Brazilian cracks Atletico Mineiro and Corinthians'.[35] They seemed to have forgotten that Neo-Gers had been playing against youngsters. Then again, maybe they got it nearly right; the words 'crack' and 'Brazilian' conjure up images of a certain part of the human anatomy, images that sum up both Neo-Gers and its supporters.

4
Money

When Boxy was sacked, the Neo-Gers board gave its reasons, which were that 'results have been disappointing and not commensurate with the level of investment that was made available'.[1] In other words, they'd allowed Boxy to spend a fortune during the summer and he'd gone out and bought a shower of duds. The amounts spent, though, were debatable, as every purchase made was announced as being for 'an undisclosed sum'. The sums quoted in the papers were sheer guesswork or came from Jabba's headquarters; The People had to be kept happy. Like sticks of rhubarb, their nurturing necessitated liberal shovelfuls of shite.

Although the initial outlay might be debated, what couldn't be questioned was the amount being paid out in wages. Details are hard to come by, but Phil Mac Giolla Bhain reckoned, in December 2017, that, between them, Alves, Candeias, Herrera and Peña were pocketing £140k per week.[2] Everybody knew that Neo-Gers were skint and relying on loans from the directors; but how long could that last?

Well, it had lasted quite a while already; over two years, in fact. The plan was that, eventually, these loans would be turned into equity, but nobody knew when that was going to be. This was how Neo-Gers avoided scrutiny under financial fair play rules, but they were going to have to get that share issue sorted out sooner rather than later. Shares, however, were to present their own problems for the club.

The Takeover Panel had decided that Honest Dave and his cronies had acted in concert to acquire a controlling interest in Neo-Gers. King being King, he appealed this decision, but the Takeover Appeal Board upheld it. He was ordered, as the leader of the concert party, to make an offer for all the shares not owned by him and his pals. The price was set at 20p per share and King had to put money in an escrow account to show that he had the wherewithal. To say he wasn't happy about it would be an understatement.

Honest Dave's answer to this was just to ignore it. The deadline for him to provide proof that he was complying with the TAB's decision came and went with King making no moves whatsoever. The Takeover Panel had no choice but to take the case to the Court of Session to force King to make the offer for those other shares. As we kept hearing, this would 'have no bearing on Rangers International Football Club Plc or The Rangers (sic) Football Club Ltd.'[3]

The case began on the 12th October, with Lord Davidson of Glen Cova appearing for King. Despite Honest Dave's earlier claims that he and the Three Bears had not acted in concert, this did not form part of Lord Davidson's case. Instead, the Counsel for the Defence contended that forcing King into complying with the Takeover Panel's ruling would be a waste of time. He based this on the argument that Honest Dave was penniless and didn't have access to the funds needed.[4] Apparently, all his assets were tied up in a family trust.[5]

As Phil Mac Giolla Bhain pointed out, this was bad news for the Neo-Gers board since the expectation all along had been that King would eventually stump up funds.[6] In fact, Honest Dave himself had been making such promises for years.[7] Surely he hadn't been lying!

Lord Davidson then claimed that forcing his client to make an offer for the rest of the Neo-Gers shares was also a waste of time by dint of the reason that nobody would sell at 20p. When the Judge, Lord Bannatyne, asked how King knew that nobody would accept this price, the Defence Counsel was rather evasive. He could only contend that there was no evidence that anybody would be prepared to take a loss of 25% on their shares.[8]

This was disingenuous in the extreme. Shares in Neo-Gers, or, rather, the holding company, TRIFC, were not trading on any exchange and were, effectively, worthless. They could, naturally, be sold privately but would only be worth what the buyer was prepared to pay. There was every chance that shareholders would jump at the opportunity to offload their shares at 20p. Certainly, Lord Davidson was right in stating that there was no evidence that shareholders would be prepared to sell. Equally, though, there was no evidence that they would not.

Incredibly, Lord Davidson went on to make the excuse that King didn't understand the '30% rule'.[9] How the hell could anyone be involved in all different businesses over the years without being aware of that aspect of business law? Even many laymen, with no experience whatsoever of business, are aware of this rule. Besides, King was not as ignorant as was being implied. As Clumps pointed out, on the same thread, he had been well aware of how many shares you needed to call an EGM.[10]

This pathetic defence was torn to shreds the next day when the Takeover Panel's lawyer, James McNeill, didn't just argue their case but produced evidence that showed King to be a liar.[11] And McNeill hadn't had to look very far for his proof; as he pointed out, most of it was in the public domain. Indeed, anybody was free to look at the Neo-Gers accounts for 2016, which claimed that King was wholly in control of New Oasis Assets Limited (NOAL).[12]

So, who was King lying to? On the one hand, he was telling the Court of Session that he was totally rooked and couldn't afford to make any kind of offer for the Neo-Gers shares that he and his cronies didn't already own. On the other, he had the Neo-Gers Board and The People, as well as the agnivores, believing that he was the rich benefactor they all craved. It was obvious to anybody with half a brain that serious questions needed to be asked. Unfortunately for The People, they can't muster half a brain between them.

On the 30th November, the Neo-Gers AGM was held at the Clyde Auditorium.[13] According to the Daily Record, the Neo-Gers Board 'faced a grilling'.[14] That was highly unlikely; since King had arrived the AGMs had been more akin to a Nuremberg Rally than Prime Minister's Question Time. Gone were the days of rat masks and hanging effigies.

Sure enough, King and his board got an easy ride, with The People accepting that they'd have to wait for a new manager and nodding sagely at Honest Dave's assurances that the financial plans were coming together. Most of the meeting, however, was taken up with demands for Celtic's ticket allocation at Ibrox to be reduced.[15] These demands were couched in terms of being upset at the behaviour of Celtic supporters.

> The fact that they are given a full stand at the expense of our supporters in the family stand is unacceptable considering how their fans behave and Celtic's actions against our club over the past several years. With the

recent incident where a flare was fired at our goalkeeper, this issue has become even more pressing.[16]

These arguments for the Celtic supporters to get less seats at Ibrox had been going on for a while. One ridiculous excuse was that, since both sets of supporters received the same allocation, then The People were being short-changed because Celtic Park had 10,000 extra seats; the Neo-Gers supporters were getting less of an allocation in *percentage* terms![17]

Mark Dingwall, of the FollowFollow website, said that it was not just the Celtic *supporters* they were concerned about:

> I think there is a groundswell among the fans that the behaviour of the Celtic support as a whole and some of their players in particular has become so outrageous in the last couple of seasons that something really needs to be done about it.[18]

Aw! The poor, wee souls were upset about Leigh Griffiths tying a Celtic scarf to their goalpost. Diddums! Amazingly, it was the Daily Record that pointed to the real reason The People wanted less Celtic supporters at Ibrox. Showing an uncharacteristic perspicacity, the DR reporter said that the Neo-Gers supporters 'have clearly had enough of their rivals gloating on Edmiston Drive'![19]

The concerns of The People were laid bare with one particular individual posing the following to Honest Dave: 'Like you, I'm from Castlemilk. I take it you went to Grange Secondary rather than St Margaret-Mary's?'[20] Actually, King attended Allan Glen's School in Glasgow's Cathedral Street; a fact easily discovered online. It was a rhetorical question, though, intended to establish, to everyone's satisfaction, that their club's chairman wasn't one of *them*.

The People, as usual, were letting their bigotry and hatred blind them to what was going on under their very noses. Trouble was headed their club's way and, yet, all they were concerned about was keeping the 'Taigs' out of Ibrox. King must have been laughing himself to sleep every night.

In December, Lord Bannatyne delivered his decision about the Takeover Panel ruling. In his written judgment, the Court of Session judge ruled that King had control over his family trusts and so had to make an offer to the other shareholders within thirty days.[21]

The Neo-Gers Managing Director, Stewart Robertson, was quick to assuage any worries that The People might have.

> It doesn't have any impact on us at all. That is an issue for Dave in terms of the shareholders.
> In terms of the day to day running of the club and the PLC and the share issue we are looking at in the future, it has no impact on that whatsoever.
> I don't believe [there will be any impact on Dave's investment]. It is an issue for Dave.
> As far as the club is concerned, we are just running as we do. It is not impacting on any decisions we are taking at all.[22]

So, it was an issue for Dave and would have no impact on Neo-Gers. But how could it not have? If King failed to comply with the Court of Session ruling, then the Cold Shoulder would come into force. This doesn't affect somebody personally, only their business dealings. And the only business dealings King had in the UK were with Neo-Gers. Despite all the protestations to the contrary, this was going to hit Neo-Gers hard. Already, they had no NOMAD, no bank would touch them with a bargepole, other than Metro Bank[23] and, as Phil Mac Giolla Bhain constantly pointed out, they had no credit line from their bank. If the Cold Shoulder was enforced, Metro Bank would have to, since it is licensed by the Financial Services Athority,[24] stop dealing with King and, consequently, with Neo-Gers.

Quite a few bloggers, and folk on Twitter, used the analogy of Honest Dave kicking a can down the street to explain his dealings with the Takeover Panel and the Court of Session. Essentially, King was just putting off the inevitable, desperately hoping that something would turn up. This explains his decision to appeal Lord Bannatyne's judgment.[25]

One thing that's harder to explain is why he was allowed to appeal. King had no legal arguments to present and all his lawyer did was regurgitate the stuff about Honest Dave having no money and nobody accepting the offer of 20p a share. It was hardly a big surprise when the appeal was thrown out.[26] The speed with which this was done only added to the puzzle of why it was allowed. Robert Fitzpatrick, commenting on my blog, had a theory that was probably close to the truth:

> With regards to having zero legal argument, clearly there is a process in place to follow even if it is a waste of time, Dave King can't claim any unfairness etc., that's the reason I think it happened, he has nowhere to go with regards to the ruling.[27]

So that was that; Honest Dave's can had reached the end of the street. All we had to do now was wait to see what was going to happen next. Some of us, however, believed that nothing at all was going to happen.[28] After everything that King had been able to slither his way out of and the SFA letting him run Neo-Gers, despite being a convicted criminal and allowing his club to keep running on fumes, it was doubtful that a mere court judgement would get in his way. A way out of the mess would be found; when it came to Neo-Gers it always was.

Rather incredibly, a way out of the whole sorry shambles presented itself in January; or so it seemed. While the transfer window was open, Neo-Gers brought in three new signings and a handful of loans, adding to their already bloated wage bill. Nobody wanted to buy any of the Neo-Gers players; and certainly not any of the Action Man's Heids that Boxy had brought in. The only one the club managed to get off the payroll was Danny Wilson, who went to American side Colorado Rapids.[29] And then came some big news.

It was Sky Sports that first broke the news: Chinese club Beijing Renhe were offering £7m for Alfredo Morelos.[30] This bid was knocked back, as was an almost immediate, increased offer of £7.5m. The reason given was that the team could not afford to lose Morelos and the decision was a football one, which took precedence over finances.[31]

There was confusion over the amounts being offered, with one source putting it at £8m.[32] The Chinese transfer window didn't close until the end of February, so there was time for more bids to be made. Sure enough, in the middle of February, Beijing Renhe bid

£9m, which Neo-Gers rejected yet again.[33] Some reports even had the Chinese club going as high as £11m, with Neo-Gers still standing firm.[34] With most folk suspecting that King would have bitten the hands off whoever ran Beijing Renhe for that amount, a nasty, Jabbaesque smell hung over the whole business.

In China, football clubs are only allowed to sign a maximum of three foreign players and there is a huge levy, which some put at 100%, on foreign signings over $7m. BBC reporter Kheredine Idessane pointed this out as early as February 1st, as well as stating that he had learned from a 'source close to Beijing Renhe' that no offer whatever had been made for Morelos.[35]

It was only a matter of hours before Idessane was forced to delete his tweet, say that he had got things wrong and then apologise to Neo-Gers.[36] The People were overjoyed, wallowing in their righteous indignation.

> Nothing has changed at the BBC they are still infested by tarrier bastards who find it impossible to report anything remotely true about us
> And yet think nothing about backing any shite that leaves the mouth of Brenda[37]

It was a strange situation. Had Neo-Gers shown Idessane proof that the bids were genuine? If they had, then why didn't they show everybody in the media? After all, there were a lot of sceptics out there. Some felt that Idessane had been got at somehow, especially since he wasn't the only one pointing out that the Chinese club already had its quota of foreign players and would hardly fork out millions for Morelos, and the same amount in tax, for a player that they couldn't use.[38]

Another thing that made no sense was Neo-Gers' reaction to these 'bids'. Why were they turning down this much-needed cash? And it certainly was needed. The 2017 Neo-Gers accounts had made plain that at least £4m was needed to see out the season. The auditors, however, were assured that NOAL, if all else failed, would be able to stump up. In fact, it's probable that the auditors wouldn't have signed off the accounts if it weren't for this reassurance.[39] But who was giving these assurances? King had had his lawyer declare, in the Court of Session, that he had no control over NOAL; so how could they be

41

relied upon? Surely if King had no control and somebody else was giving these assurances, they might well change their minds. It is doubtful that the auditors would have signed off the accounts if King could give no guarantees. He was playing a dangerous game.

These astronomical bids supposedly coming from the Orient would have helped Neo-Gers, and King, no end. The only possible conclusion to be drawn from Neo-Gers turning the bids down is that they were a complete fantasy. Probably Jabba ate too much Chinese food one evening and had to 'reach for the Rennie'. That, no doubt, got the wheels in his head turning.

Pick up a newspaper in Scotland, or go on one of those newspapers' websites, and you'll invariably come across a 'good news' story about Neo-Gers. One such story came along on the 7th February. Stewart Robertson was announcing that Neo-Gers had a new banker and, not only that, the club had 'been granted an overdraft of "modest millions"'.[40] Gary Ralston, whose article it was, said that he understood that 'the facility is less than £3 million'. Robertson stressed, though, that Dave 'Impecuniosity' King and his fellow 'investors' (i.e. lenders) would still be there to pick up the slack.[41]

That appeared to be great news for The People; their new club was finally getting its act together financially. No longer could Phil Mac Giolla Bhain come out with his saying regarding credit lines and banks. The rest of Ralston's article, however, was rather more disconcerting. He said, 'The overdraft will be secured against Edmiston House and the Albion car park'.[42] That didn't sound right. Who ever heard of an overdraft needing security?

Phil Mac Giolla Bhain's *Rugger Guy* was on the case, albeit ten days later, telling us the facts on what we suspected, that Close Brothers 'do not provide overdrafts, they are lenders.'[43] He went on to let us know that this was a lender of last resort, with Wonga-like interest rates and all manner of punitive clauses in the contract. To sum up, it wasn't good news for Neo-Gers after all; it was a sign of desperation.

And if that wasn't bad enough, on the very last day of February, Honest Dave's appeal was thrown out.[44] There was now no other avenue left for him; he either had to offer to buy those shares or face the Cold Shoulder or even prison.

What Ever Happened To?

After the 'glamour' of the Florida Cup it was back to the nitty-gritty of the Scottish Premiership. They might not have the luxury of playing against kids anymore, but at least the match officials were on their side and nobody questioned their choice of singing material. All-in-all, it probably felt good to be home.

The first match came on the 24th January at Ibrox against Aberdeen. Neo-Gers struggled to find the goal, apart from one shot from Morelos that managed to go in. The Aberdeen goalie got carried off injured in the second half, which induced Bobby 'Ibrox Season Ticket' Madden to point to the spot. This customary penalty helped Neo-Gers secure all three points.[1]

Penalties also played a part in the next game, against Ross County in Dingwall. Neo-Gers won 2-1, with Ross County getting a penalty, almost on the final whistle, for a hand-ball incident. County, however, should have had another penalty earlier on in the match, when young Master Bates stopped a header with his arm.[2]

Embarrassingly, when Jason Cummings scored Neo-Gers' second goal, some of The People ran onto the pitch, in what Chris McLaughlin at the BBC called, 'a mini pitch invasion'.[3] Strangely, whenever supporters of Neo-Gers' opponents do that, there are strongly-worded statements on the website and letters to the SFA. Apparently, though, it's okay for them to do it.

When talking about the Aberdeen game, the BBC referred to 'Graeme Murty's new-look side'[4]; and it *was* new-look. Neo-Gers had been busy in the January window. They had signed Declan John, Greg Docherty and Glenn Middleton and punted Danny Wilson to American side, Colorado Rapids. All of these transactions were for the usual 'undisclosed fee', which could have meant anything and left the agnivores free to make up whatever figures suited the agenda.

They also brought in four loan players: Sean Goss, Jamie Murphy, Jason Cummings and Russell Martin. There were also players loaned out: Myles Beerman, Jordan Thompson, Ryan Hardie and the consistently useless Carlos Peña. They were rather fortunate to get rid of the latter; Boxy still saw something in Peña that nobody else could and welcomed him to Cruz Azul with open arms. The last we heard of him, he was being booed by his own team's supporters while being stretchered off.[5]

While it might seem like a good thing that Murty was able to bring in his own signings and loan players, it actually heaped more pressure on his shoulders. Up to the winter break, he was allowed a bit of leeway by The People and the agnivores, since he was stuck with Boxy's band of losers. Now, he was going to have to prove himself with players he was responsible for.

In those first two games, Murty hadn't had to prove anything; the referee was there to make sure Neo-Gers won. The next game was no different. In the Scottish Cup it's always been the case that Rangers, and then Neo-Gers, get drawn at home. To cover up this obvious fix, they're sometimes given away games; but always against lower-league opposition. This year was no exception and, in the Fourth Round, they were pitted against the Highland-League team Fraserburgh.

Even this match needed the intervention of the referee. Fraserburgh gave as good as they got for fifteen minutes, and then Neo-Gers got a penalty for nothing. Jason Holt tripped over the ball in the Fraserburgh area and the referee immediately pointed to the spot. After that it was just a case of using the tactics Neo-Gers employed when they were in the lower leagues; wait for the part-time players to get tired. With two more goals in the second half, Neo-Gers progressed to the next round.[6]

At the start of February, it became clear that Neo-Gers still had a problem with stringing together a decent series of wins. At least they could manage three-in-a-row these days, but not much further than that. The latest run was brought to an abrupt end when Hibs came to Ibrox and won 2-1.

It would be difficult to imagine which element of this defeat hurt and angered The People most. Morelos was denied a goal for being offside, while Hibs' winning goal was a last-minute penalty. A penalty, against Neo-Gers, at Ibrox. Such a thing was unheard of.[7] What probably saddened and irritated The People the most, though, was that their perennial hate-figure, Neil Lennon, was leaving Ibrox, yet again, with bragging rights.

During the rest of February, though, Neo-Gers managed to put together a run of wins, including against Partick Thistle, Hamilton, Hearts and St Johnstone in the league. In the Scottish Cup Fifth Round, they defeated Ayr United 6-1. Managing five wins in a row, of course, meant that they were 'coming down the road' again. It doesn't take much to make The People positive and overconfident.

The agnivores were getting a bit overexcited too. The thing was, there was a league match coming up against Celtic on the 11th of March and The People and the agnivores were convinced that their big moment had come: Neo-Gers were going to win. And that wasn't the only thing; the way things stood, Neo-Gers could be equal on points with Celtic by the middle of March. The fabled '55' could well be back on.

What was getting them all orgasmic was the fact that Neo-Gers' victory at McDiarmid Park meant that they were only six points behind the league-leaders.[8] Celtic were due to play Dundee the next evening, but the heavy snow caused the match to be called off.[9] All the calculators, abacuses and fingers (six on each Govan hand) were out immediately and it transpired that, if Neo-Gers beat Celtic then they would be only three points behind. All they had to do then was beat Kilmarnock on the 17th and Robert was your dad's brother. Of course, they had to hope that the Dundee game wouldn't be rescheduled too quickly, and they might only be on equal points for 24 hours but that was good enough. The hope was that Celtic would become utterly demoralised and throw away the rest of the season.

The Daily Record did its usual job of building up what it called the 'Old Firm' derby, even though such a beast no longer existed. All the old clichés were in full flow: you can't predict the outcome of an 'Old Firm' match etc. To underline this, and to pander to the Big Lie, references were constantly made to old Celtic and Rangers matches;[10] as if they mattered anymore. Still, these articles helped The People to remember the good old days and to build the hope that they might come back some day.

These wanders down memory lane were taken to almost ridiculous extremes. Such a piece was headlined, 'Whatever happened to Rangers Superleague Formula team?'[11] If you've never heard of this, don't worry, the Daily Record's poll on just this issue proved that hardly anybody had. It shows how 'high profile' the whole thing was. The DR explained that it was 'Devised as a new brand of high-speed

45

motor racing the series introduced team sponsorship by some of the biggest football clubs in the world.'[12]

To my mind, there's no spectator sport more boring than watching cars going round and round a track; even watching a game of dominoes would be more exciting. Still, *chacun à son goût*. The DR provided pictures of Walter Smith, and others, posing with a racing car, surrounded by a gaggle of the type of female you rarely see at Ibrox; i.e. attractive. Like all seemed-like-a-good-idea-at-the-time enterprises this one was doomed to failure. Looking back, the involvement of Setanta hardly augured well.

The Daily Record's article on this venture hardly inspires confidence in its veracity. It says,

> The Ibrox men were the first British club to enter the fast lane for the inaugural season of the sport in 2008 just a month after winning the SPL title.[13]

Oops! Maybe they think, like The People, that they *should* have won the league that year, but the cheating authorities wouldn't extend the season to October.

If that sentence was calculated to suck up to The People, one later in the article most definitely was not.

> However, the sixth round of the 2009 season, in Jarama, Spain, proved to be the last race involving Rangers with the club getting out of the series before it crashed and burned.[14]

Er…did that mean the series 'crashed and burned' or was it referring to Rangers?

Anyway, enough history. Back to 2018 and, before the Celtic match, there was the little formality of a Scottish Cup Quarter-Final. With Neo-Gers' seven potential rivals coming from the Premiership and Championship, it was time for a home tie. Falkirk were drawn to make the trip to Ibrox. Considering they were floundering about at the bottom of the Championship, Falkirk had done well to make it this far in the Scottish Cup. Needless to say, though, Neo-Gers steamrollered them to a 4-1 defeat.[15]

This, of course, made the agnivores all the more convinced that Neo-Gers were going to beat Celtic and a title race would be on. Gordon Parks opined,

> It may be a stretch to suggest Celtic fans are worried but there is a quiet concern that they're about to confront an improved Ibrox side.
> The tit-for-tat last week has been cranked up a few levels higher than normal because a routine win over Rangers is no longer the expectancy under Brendan Rodgers.[16]

Barry Ferguson, meanwhile, said, 'Rangers can give Celtic the fright of their lives and it's all down to the brilliant job Graeme Murty has done'.[17] This confidence affected The People as well and they started to believe that the upcoming match was somewhat of a formality.

> Murty has played two against Rodgers and drawn both of them. That shows that the Celtic manager isn't all that and his team are not what they are cracked up to be.'[18]

> Rodgers is a worried man ahead of the trip to Ibrox and that's why he's started the mind games.
> Rangers will show him on Sunday that we are as good at home as we are on the road. I've rarely been as confident of beating Celtic who are being exposed as a bang average side.[19]

The People on Neo-Gers media were more forthright, if less grammatically correct.

> time to put these manky fenian bastards in there place.[20]

> 4-3 us written all over it.[21]

In fact, so confident were The People that they could take the time to concern themselves with other matters. They had seen on the telly that Arsenal had blue lines on the pitch when they were playing Manchester City. Of course, they wanted the same at Ibrox.[22] It's always been a major source of annoyance to The People that God made grass green instead of blue.

Also a major source of annoyance to The People is…well…practically anything, really. Something seemed to have annoyed the *Union Bears* and they were ready to march about it. Either that or they simply couldn't wait for July to come. They produced a flyer to advertise their walk, saying, 'The Union Bears have organised a fans march to Ibrox before this Sunday's match against the fenians.'[23] And a logo was made especially for the march and the flyer, which showed someone, wearing a green top, lying on the ground while holding a hand up in an attempt to stop the other figure kicking him in the face. The legend beneath said, 'GOOD NIGHT GREEN WHITE'.[24]

Supposedly, the police were looking into this, but nothing transpired. The People had no idea why these folk were marching either, but they were keen to support them. They anticipated trouble if the police were heavy-handed, which they assumed they would be. After all, Police Scotland was under the control of the terrorist-loving, Republican-supporting and Pope-worshipping SNP![25]

And then came the big day. Nothing had happened yet to diminish the confidence of The People and the agnivores. Gordon Parks, in the Sunday Mail, was certain how things were going to go, saying, 'Celtic skipper Scott Brown is poster boy for Scottish football's mediocrity and Greg Docherty can get the better of him'.[26] Now that was taking things too far. It made it seem as if Scottish football was nothing without Neo-Gers.

The *Union Bears* had their march, with black clothing, hidden faces, drums, flares, union flags and banners with that new logo of theirs.[27] There didn't appear to be any violence, especially since they were accompanied, and protected, by some of Glasgow's finest, who smiled as if they were on a day out.[28] One couldn't help wondering if some of their brother officers were under those face-covering scarves.

Refereeing the match was Willie Collum, which, if the comments in the Evening Times were to be believed, the supporters of neither side were happy about.[29] The fourth official was Andrew Dallas, with Andrew McWilliam and part-time Tory MP Douglas Ross as linesmen. Apart from Dallas, it seemed a neutral enough line-up and, as fourth official, Dallas couldn't do much harm.

48

It was an exciting match that went back and forward; Neo-Gers scoring, Celtic equalising, Neo-Gers scoring again, Celtic equalising again. And then, Celtic were down to ten men and Tom Rogic had to make way for Jack Hendry in defence. Only a few minutes later, Rodgers took off James Forrest and sent on Odsonne Edouard. The latter was barely on the pitch before he scored Celtic's third. And that was how the match ended; 3-2 to Celtic and yet another Ibrox defeat for Neo-Gers at the hands of Brendan Rodgers.[30]

It was an outcome that the agnivores had not even allowed themselves to consider. All their talk was about Neo-Gers being just three points behind Celtic and being equal on points once they had beaten Kilmarnock. The alternative was too awful to think about, but it had happened. Celtic were now nine points ahead with a game in hand.[31]

Murty was convinced that the loss was his own team's fault. He said, 'The people on the pitch had more than enough experience and opportunity to go and win that and we've managed to throw it away.'[32] In fact, the only reason that Neo-Gers managed to score at all was down the walking disaster area that is Boyata. Both Neo-Gers goals were caused by his mistakes and not by any great play by the Ibrox team. If Murty had really looked at the game, he would have realised that his team was still not good enough to mount any kind of challenge to Celtic.

Much was made of how Morelos missed a sitter that could have given Neo-Gers a draw, but the truth is that he shouldn't even have been on the pitch. He committed foul after foul throughout the match and didn't get so much as a yellow card. Equally, Declan John should have been shown a straight red in the first half for a two-footed lunge.[33]

Now, the referee can't be expected to see everything, which is why he has two assistants running the lines. If the assistant chooses not to tell the referee what has happened, then an incident can easily go unpunished. Such was the case with that two-footed lunge by Declan John. It happened practically right in front of Douglas Ross, but he chose to ignore it.

There is a line in *War and Peace* which goes something like, He had a face that women wanted to mother and men wanted to punch. Ross has that kind of face, except women probably want to punch him as well. The only reason he managed to be elected MP for

Moray was that he was the beneficiary of tactical voting to keep the SNP from winning the seat. He's certainly not been much of a parliamentarian, failing to turn up for crucial debates and votes.

He looks like he was the kind of child that is the bane of the lives of both teachers and fellow pupils. You know the type; always having their hand in the air, shouting, 'Miss! Miss!' to tell the teacher about somebody doing something trivial, like talking. He still looks the type that's desperate to get others into trouble and his performance at Ibrox confirmed this.

The incident involving Jozo Simunovic and Alfredo Morelos happened quickly. Simunovic's arm caught Morelos, who went down as if he'd been shot and then thrashed about like a landed trout. It's difficult to find any video footage of what happened because all attention became focused on the aftermath. Instead of simply waving his flag to draw the referee's attention, Ross went back to his childhood and started shouting, 'Red card! Red card!'[34] All that was missing was the 'Miss! Miss!'

Willie Collum didn't even bother speaking with Ross; he just did as he was told and flashed a red card at Simunovic. In normal circumstances, it isn't an assistant's place to tell the referee what to do. His job is to draw the referee's attention to incidents and leave the man in charge to decide what to do. Quite often the referee will consult the players as well before reaching a decision. The whole business was an extreme embarrassment for all concerned. As Brian McClair put it,

> This morning 3 guys in Scotland arrived at their place of work, got changed into their Black uniforms and started their shift, soon one decided to be the star of the show, another decided in one instance that he was going to be famous...[35]

At the end of the match, the Ibrox bouncers were out in force again to guard the goalposts. They needn't have worried, though, since Leigh Griffiths was out injured and hadn't taken part in the game. He was, however, among the spectators in the Broomloan Stand and he still managed to rile The People. Someone handed him an Irish tricolour flag, which he waved enthusiastically. Of course, this image ended up in the papers.

Strangely, the media reported that it was members of the Tartan Army that were upset by the flag-waving.[36] This is a phrase that often crops up in the paper, but what does it even mean? The impression given is of a large group of football supporters that follow no club but sit around in their *C U Jimmy* hats, waiting for the next Scotland game. Quite obviously, it's a load of shite.

The members of the so-called Tartan Army that were upset were of the ilk of this character:

> Celebrate yes, but this once again is a step too far. I am a Rangers (sic) fan and a Scotland fan, once again I question my support for this player, and that should not be.[37]

Others of the same stamp had more to say on the matter:

> I don't know if he has Irish connections or what religion he is but if he is a Scottish Protestant acting like that then I for one would gladly piss on his grave when he snuffs it. Imagine that traitor watching your back in a war zone FFS![38]

> Given his allegiance to Hibs and Celtic I'm guessing he is a rattler of the beads.[39]

In truth, what they were annoyed about was not that he was waving the flag of a foreign country; it was more to do with the particular country whose flag he was waving. It was bigotry, pure and simple, that caused the outrage, as is obvious from the comments above.

Griffiths took the mickey out of himself by posting a *Still Game*-themed joke, where Jack and Victor ask him what part of Ireland he's from, to which Griffiths replies, 'Leith'.[40] That, however, made no difference to the bigots; they wanted his head. Almost unnoticed amid all the furore over a flag, Griffiths had also tied his trademark scarf to a rail.[41]

While The People were getting all riled about a flag, Celtic supporters had found a new catchphrase. Neo-Gers has its own TV channel, called Rangers (sic) TV, which is available to folk outside the UK. When a match is over, Neo-Gers supporters can pay to watch the game all over again. Highlights are available on the Neo-Gers website free for a limited time. The match commentators are Tom Miller and Hugh Burns, whose screaming and yelling even gets on the nerves of some of The People.[42]

On this occasion, they were more excited than usual since their team had actually managed to score two goals. Neo-Gers were leading 2-1 when Scott Brown made a spectacular pass, just before being fouled, that put Moussa Dembélé in on goal. Wes Foderingham came rushing out of his goal toward Dembélé, allowing the latter to punt the ball over the goalkeeper's head and into the net. Hugh Burns yelled excitedly the now classic phrase, 'What's the goalie daein', Tom? What's the goalie doin'?'[43]

Almost immediately, the phrase was all over Twitter and other social media. Within days, it had appeared as graffiti on walls and even on tee-shirts. It was the sort of gift that only appears once in a blue moon and everybody certainly made the most of it.

A week later, The People were still trying to come to terms with the fact that things hadn't exactly gone to plan. That plan had been that, with a win against Kilmarnock, Neo-Gers would be equal on points with Celtic; a St Patrick's Day gift The People would have loved to hand over. Obviously, the first part of the plan had come untangled and the second, unfortunately for them, did the same.

Neo-Gers were beaten 1-0 at home to Kilmarnock. To add insult to injury, it was Kris Boyd that scored the only goal of the match.[44] To look at Boyd, you wouldn't believe he'd be capable of scoring goals. In the picture in the *Guardian*,[45] he looks, especially in comparison to the Neo-Gers players, like a grandad, huffing and puffing as he tries to play football with the grandweans in the park. It was an embarrassment to be beaten by a goal from this fat lump.

Besides, Boyd wasn't sticking to the script. Remember years ago, when Sooperally and Ian Durrant played for Kilmarnock during their twilight years? Both of them refused to score against Rangers and had to be taken off. Boyd didn't just play for Rangers; he played for Neo-Gers as well. What the hell was he doing scoring against them? It just wasn't right!

With that Kilmarnock game, Murty had used up any goodwill The People still possessed for him. There was no appetite anymore for him to take over permanently; they needed a *real* manager.[46] Noises were already being made about enticing Stevie Clarke from Kilmarnock.[47] If he'd any sense, though, he wouldn't go anywhere near the manager's job at Ibrox. That job is like the Defence against the Dark Arts teaching post in *Harry Potter*, it's cursed

6
Hollow Inside

The main theme of all these books on Neo-Gers has been the impact of the Big Lie. If it had been accepted that Rangers had died, and a new team had taken its place, things would have gone a lot more smoothly. It was the insistence that it was 'still Rangers' that caused all the problems that Neo-Gers constantly faced. It was the fault of the football authorities, the media and, of course, The People themselves, for not facing up to the truth.

Celtic under Fergus McCann should have provided a template for rebuilding. It was a tough time for Celtic supporters, watching Rangers winning everything while their own club balanced the books and slowly built for the future. It was painful at the time, but all Celtic supporters would now agree that it was worth it in the end.

Neo-Gers were actually in a better position than Celtic had been in 1994. As a completely new club it had shed all of Rangers' debts (apart from some football ones) and was starting with a clean slate. Slowly building for the future should have been easier too since they were starting over in the bottom tier and didn't have to shell out millions to maintain a place in the top division.

The People, and the agnivores, however, demanded immediate success. All opposition had to be crushed underfoot and the club had to get to the top tier as quickly as possible. Once in the top division, the expectation, nay, the demand, was that the team should overhaul Celtic and start European football almost at once.

Both Mark Warburton (Warbs) and Pedro Caixinha (Boxy) warned that success couldn't be achieved overnight and spoke about taking time to build a team. Arrogantly, however, The People and the agnivores demanded that their team immediately overhaul Celtic. This was 'Rangers' we were talking about; why should they wait? Money should be no object and it didn't matter if Ibrox stadium was falling apart at the seams; all that concerned The People was that they should be top of the heap.

Even now, in 2018, lessons hadn't been learned. In April, Honest Dave was telling The People that they'd be welcoming a new manager next season.

> However, on the managerial front I emphasise that the Board fully recognises the need for sustained stability in this area of the Club. Whoever is appointed must be able to meet the unique challenges of managing Rangers (sic) and ensuring immediate success.[1]

This might well just have been grandstanding; it was part of a sales pitch for season tickets, after all. The title of the sales campaign, 'We are Rangers', however, showed clearly that the Big Lie was still paramount. Besides, if immediate success was promised, then that's what The People would be demanding. Neo-Gers were already up to their ears in debt and it seriously looked as if the new club was going to end up going the same way as the old one. But finance wasn't the only effect that the Big Lie had.

Bigotry, belligerence and hatred have always been associated with The People, but, ever since Rangers went into liquidation and Charles Green started up his new club, it's been highly noticeable that they've become more bigoted, more belligerent and more hate-filled than before. This has been yet another consequence of the Big Lie. They've been bitter as hell since 2012.

The *Vanguard Bears* website, a staunch bastion of bitterness and bile, summed up the general feeling among The People. They were talking, as usual, about how hard-done-by they were and how Celtic, and Peter Lawwell in particular, were trying to punish them further.

> It seems that Rangers being demoted to the bottom division, losing a squad of full international players, being fined while in Administration, being penalised points in the 2011/2012 season, with the result effectively handing Celtic both a free run for 5 years at

the title, and 5 years riches of the champions league is not enough.[2]

For nearly six years now, this nonsense had been peddled in the media as the truth. Since The People have been led to believe that they're still supporting the same team, then it stands to reason that they're going to blame all and sundry for everything that happened. While normal folk realise that starting over in the bottom tier, losing players etc. were consequences of liquidation, The People have been convinced that liquidation never happened. With that in mind, it becomes obvious to them that their club was the victim of a vicious conspiracy.

This conspiracy isn't just confined to the Scottish football authorities, or even just to Scotland. *Vanguard Bears* reckon that

> former Celtic Chairman (and friend of Dawn Primarolo) John Reid's friends at HMRC moved the goalposts on tax, at the same time that Govt owned Lloyds bank, were attempting to strangle the club.[3]

Even when they admit that David Murray was to blame for the financial problems, their concern is that 'he left us vulnerable to forces looking for an excuse to damage or kill Rangers'.[4] There's just no arguing with that kind of delusion.

Since The People believe that Celtic, its directors and its supporters, is responsible for everything that happened to Rangers, and is happening to Neo-Gers, they are constantly on the lookout for ways to denigrate what they see as 'the enemy'. Anything will do; even ancient history.[5] Rewriting this history is part-and-parcel of their agenda.

> The part played by Maley's comments regards the 1909 'Hampden Riot' final and the majority of his players malingering on the pitch at the end of the replay.[6]

Anybody that knows anything about what happened at Hampden in 1909 knows that both sets of supporters rioted, believing that Celtic and Rangers were trying to rip them off. And those players 'malingering' were just as confused as everybody else about what was happening. Both clubs had to stump up for the damage and the record shows that nobody won that year's Scottish Cup.

Not content with trying to rewrite history, The People try to recount every instance where Celtic supporters got into trouble with the law. They show no sense of irony or even self-awareness when it comes to this desperate trawling of the past, as these two examples illustrate.

> IRA song book in Manchester, various broken seats and numerous incidents involving violence, the most shameful saw a young kid hit on the head with half a brick and required hospital treatment. More included service station attacks on innocent people.[7]

> A Celtic fan has been sentenced to four years in jail by a Spanish court for two drink-fuelled Champions League attacks.
> The teenage Hoops supporter battered two men with beer jugs ahead of a match against Barcelona.[8]

It would be hilarious if it weren't so pathetic. In fact, it is hilarious *and* pathetic. And if you think that's bad, there's even more. Here is a tweet from somebody calling himself Mr. Bluenose:

> Are you going to run a story on this then, No, thought not, it's only anti rangers story's you tend to right, but then again, your a bigot @AngelaHaggerty[9]

He appends a tweet, and a photo, from the Twitter account First Glasgow, which says,

> This is the shock reaction of our cleaners when they saw what was left for them on a number 2 that serviced the Parkhead area, Saturday.
> We ask that the fans of Celtic FC stop defecating on our vehicles after the game, otherwise we will have to withdraw the service on match days.[10]

57

The problem with that is that the account Mr. Blue is quoting from is, in fact, a parody account and has nothing at all to do with the *real* First Bus Glasgow.[11] Okay, that's maybe just one moron, but there are plenty of others, especially on the *followfollow* website.

On the 27th of February, Neo-Gers' game against St Johnstone went ahead. The next evening's matches were all postponed because of the heavy snow, including Celtic's game against Dundee. Some of The People were quick to condemn Celtic supporters' reactions to this news as showing a marked insanity.

> Well, I'll be damned. Our game postponed tonight while Sevco's went ahead. SPFL corrupt to the core.[12]

> One of the many brain donors from the east[13]

> They're more to be pitied than scorned.[14]

These were just a couple of the comments on the website, laughing at and condemning the 'stupid Taigs'. Unfortunately, the screenshot presented was from the Twitter account of *Kerrydale Meltdown* (@KerryFail), which, rather obviously, is another parody account, run by one of The People themselves.[15] It was like somebody quoting Billy 'Burger' King and presenting it as the view of a real Neo-Gers supporter. (Even though it sometimes is!)

Other commenters tried to bolster the agenda by providing links and screenshots of real Celtic supporters. On one of these, the masonic symbol was placed there by yet another Neo-Gers supporter.[16] And then there was the screenshot of a tweet by *Kevin*, saying to STV's Raman Bhardwaj,

> Raman these cancellations are nothing more than an SFA conspiracy to cancel Celtics games and allow sevco to close the gap!!![17]

Rather conveniently, the commenter posting the screenshot omitted the reply that *Kevin* made to one of The People:

It's a joke ya rocket.[18]

Unfortunately, it's not all hilarity. The *Vanguard Bears* are still banging on about things like cheap loans from the Co-Op Bank, even though that particular issue was dealt with at Westminster, with the Government stating that any such arrangement was between the bank and its customer. Then there's the stale, old arguments about land deals.

> The forever excellent footballtaxhavens blog has for many years, via FOI's, been uncovering a number of questionable transactions and local government support for Celtic which has saved millions of pounds for Celtic, that other competing clubs have not been allowed.
> Again, the appetite within the media, and agencies in a position to challenge these transactions has been remarkably low.[19]

This, yet again, is a complete lie. The DUP raised this matter a couple of years ago with the European Commission and sparked an enquiry. Nothing came of this since the enquiry could find no evidence of wrongdoing. That, however, isn't good enough for The People; what they want is their own placemen to investigate, with Celtic's guilt a foregone conclusion.

We're all familiar with *PZJ*, the character who constantly sent out FOI requests from his bedsit in Belfast, desperately trying to build a case that Celtic had been the recipient of state aid. As we know, his efforts were in vain and he and his DUP cronies were sent home with their tails between their legs. *PZJ*, however, wasn't one for giving up that easily.

His latest 'discovery' was that Celtic Park was falling to pieces.[20] He wasn't the only one; some clown with a right-wing blog, whose only other post was extolling the virtues of Enoch Powell's 'Rivers of Blood' speech, had contacted the Health and Safety Executive on the strength of a few photographs.[21] Meanwhile, somebody on FollowFollow had this contribution:

> It is built on top of an old mine, they had to pump in over 100 ton of concrete before they could begin building it. It

also sits within a blast zone of the local distillery. There was a lot of dirty deals done with the Labour government who controlled the Glasgow City Council at the time to get it all pushed through.[22]

Er…wait a minute. Isn't the usual narrative one of Glasgow City Council selling prime land to Celtic on the cheap? Now, suddenly, the whole area was a disaster waiting to happen; a place that nobody in their right mind would want to buy, whatever the price. There's nothing like undermining your own argument.

But, wait. *PZJ* had another issue up his sleeve. He had documentary proof that Celtic had not just received special favours from Glasgow Council, but hard cash from the Scottish Government.[23] In fact, the money had been paid to the Celtic FC Foundation; a charity.[24] *PZJ*, however, saw no difference between a charity bearing Celtic's name and Celtic itself. And just to confirm that he's an absolute lunatic, he had the following to say,

> Bheast FC (that's Celtic, by the way) have a history of taking from charitable public payments were (sic) no receipts or evidence of work carried out.[25]

This from a character whose old team was censured by the Scottish Charity Regulator for stealing charity money.[26] Not that The People would worry about that any; it was a *modus operandi* after their own hearts. Some of them have been known to sell poppy badges to line their own pockets.[27]

PZJ also happens to be a bigot, who has been banned from Twitter umpteen times and has to keep starting up new accounts. His latest name for Celtic supporters, 'descendants of the wonder crop failure',[28] shows what a despicable wretch he is. Like others of his ilk, however, he tries to accuse the ones he hates of being bigots. This is standard practice with The People.

Everyone is aware of how Celtic FC was founded, but The People try to twist the intentions of Brother Walfrid into something sinister. We've all heard of *Souperism* as operated in Ireland during the Great Famine, but it was still a concern long after the Famine was over. Some Protestant churches still continued the practice, while others, scared of being accused of it, refused to feed starving Catholics. Either way, it meant that destitute, Irish Catholics in Glasgow were left without any measure of support.

Brother Walfrid's initiative was a necessity to provide sustenance for the poor of the parish, but that's not the way The People tell it.

> Can anyone access bro walfrid's 'mission statement'. Where he talks about it being 'bad enough those young catholic fellows having to work with Protestants, but having to spend their leisure time with them could lead to apostasy'. It was quoted in a book about the 'old firm', but any reference to walfrid's statement seems to have disappeared from the internet.
>
> Celtc football club founded for one reason and one reason only to keep RCs away from Protestants, and sow the seeds of bigotry.[29]

This religious bigotry, which has always been a part of the People's lives, has taken a rather sinister turn since Rangers died. It's become mixed up with the belief that Rangers was the victim of some nefarious conspiracy. And, worryingly, it's also become mixed up with the concerns of the Ulster Unionists and, through them, the Orange Order.

The Protestant Ascendancy in Northern Ireland has near enough had its day and, like white supremacists did in South Africa, many Ulster Unionists find it difficult to accept. South African supremacists couldn't abide the idea of being equal with blacks, so called them 'Communists', 'terrorists' and 'destroyers'. Ulster Unionists are now of the same mindset. Their 'enemies', however, are not blacks, but Catholics.

The People not only stand firm with their Ulster 'brothers'; many of them actually *are* Unionists from Ulster.[30] The result of this is that The People believe that Catholics are to blame for all the evils in the world; especially for what happened to Rangers and what, apparently, is being done to Neo-Gers. But their hatred goes much deeper than that.

The *Vanguard Bears* website is mostly about Neo-Gers, but their motto, 'Defending Our Traditions' means much more. As they explain,

> Established in 2007, Vanguard Bears are a group of Loyalist & Unionist Rangers (sic) supporters, whose aims are to ensure that the good standing and unionist

61

tradition of THE quintessential British Club is maintained, and to support the Protestant Unionist Loyalist community in Scotland, Ulster and beyond.[31]

They go on,

> Moral and financial support has been given to the loyal people of Ulster in their fight against violent Irish Republicanism – our members have also donated thousands of pounds towards the upkeep of the Twaddell Peace Camp, and to assist in the payment of severe & unwarranted fines handed out to protestors.[32]

There is a recurring theme on most of The People's websites that what they call the Protestant Unionist Loyalist (PUL) 'community' is under attack. In Scotland, it would be difficult to apply this term to anyone but Orangemen, but the likes of *Vanguard Bears* are undaunted. To their minds, the only folk entitled to call themselves 'Protestants' are Neo-Gers-supporting members of the Orange Order. This conflation enables them to maintain that Protestantism itself is under attack.

Another mob in the same vein, but more proactive in a decidedly belligerent fashion, is *Imperial Bears*. This lot, like *Vanguard Bears*, have a mission statement, part of which is,

> Imperial Bears has been set up as a vehicle to protect and defend our community in the face of adversity, and maintain our glorious union. We aim to publicise any crimes against our community, highlight any discrimination suffered by our community, and campaign for parity! We hope to engage with as many PUL community members as possible, and ensure that apathy does not become our downfall.[33]

Whoever runs the website employs a pretty loose definition of the word 'crimes'. Cat Boyd, the well-known Scottish Socialist, for example, is classed as a 'Protestant hater' because she cited Bernadette Devlin as a hero.[34] The comedian and TV presenter,

Hardeep Singh Kohli, is another 'Protestant hater' because he compared the Israeli army invading Gaza to the trashing of Manchester by The People.[35] And Angela Haggerty is guilty of the same crime by virtue of her brother posting on Twitter that he was 'listenin' tae Republican Music'.[36] It's hardly surprising that 'To this date, not one arrest has been made relating to these serious, religiously aggravated hate crimes.'[37]

Obviously, there's a thick vein of insanity running through this website; it is also riddled with hypocrisy. Anyone familiar with this mob, or who read my account of them in *Damned Agnivores*, will be astonished at the lack of irony and self-awareness in this statement about journalist, Andrew Whittaker, looking for details of politicians who were in the Orange Order:

> This campaign now looks to be sinister in its origins. To actively seek members of the Order for the crime of being in the Order is bad enough but to induce others & request their personal details & locations so that they can contact & possibly worse pass on these details to others who are not benevolent towards the organisation is actually frightening.[38]

To those not familiar with *Imperial Bears*, the above is *their* usual *modus operandi*: finding out personal details about people and then getting in touch with their employers to try to get them sacked. If their victim has a business, The People are encouraged to boycott it and write negative reviews on the business website. There have even been vague threats made to folk's families. And yet, they've got the gall to condemn somebody else when they think he's doing the same.

As anyone could tell the *Vanguard Bears*, the *Imperial Bears* and the rest of The People, the best way to defend Protestantism and stop it dying out would be to go to church. That, however, seems to be a step too far. Besides, all the churches are probably being run by Catholics; after all, everything else is.

> Why is our country full of tarriers? Why is our media full of tarriers? Why is our government full of tarriers? Why are all our celebrities tarriers?

63

Go forth and multiply. It's what they do. That is their indoctrination. Rhats.[39]
Everything that is wrong with our club and country from top to bottom....and we let it happen...[40]

So, why isn't this bigoted paranoia challenged in the media, as well as all the sectarian singing and chanting it engenders? The sports desks at Scotland's papers might all be dancing to Jabba's tune, but that doesn't explain why ordinary journalists don't follow this stuff up. The answer is that all newspapers in Scotland, bar one, and the TV and radio channels all support us remaining part of the United Kingdom. Unfortunately, the *zeitgeist* in the UK has taken a decidedly racist turn.

We've all heard and read the stories about folk being beaten up on buses in England and Wales for having the nerve to speak in another language. Muslims are frequently targeted with violence and even the Government has been trying to get rid of folk that came here from the Caribbean when they were children.[41] On top of all that we're now committed to leaving the EU due to people voting in a referendum for mostly racist reasons. Even Enoch Powell is now being lauded as a great prophet.[42]

While we've all been waiting for The People to catch up with the 21st Century, the 21st Century has actually moved backwards to accommodate them. As long as we're a part of the UK, then The People have justification for their bigotry and hatred, since it's become part of a bigger movement. Not surprisingly, the *Imperial Bears* class the SNP as 'Protestant haters' as well.[43]

One character, on the FollowFollow website, summed up the feelings of many, if not most, of The People a few hours before Neo-Gers faced Celtic in the Scottish Cup semi-final. It needs to be read in full to get the full force of its hate-fueled, bigoted insanity.

Let's see this game in proper perspective. It was never just about the football, it never was and never will be. Let's not kid ourselves it's just about us or them winning. It is much bigger than that, it is really about two different visions; our vision is about continuity, history and traditions. It is about being British and Scottish with Her Majesty as Head of State and head of the

Anglican/Protestant church. It is about being free thinkers, an enlightened and educated people not trapped by the dictates of a foreign potentate. Yes, we are indeed the people.

Their vision is dark and dangerous. It is about chaos, rebellion, dissent, militant Republicanism. It is Irish nationalism, socialist thinking and extreme intolerance. Hatred of all things British, from Queen Elizabeth to the local state school is their trade mark.

As we see the pictures broadcast from Hampden, the flags and banners will tell it all.

Off the field, we have surrendered too much for so little. Our institutions have been undermined and in many cases the rebels have taken control from local government to the Scottish Parliament. Scotland voted to remain in Europe whereas the Scottish unionists voted rightly to get out. This was at last some evidence that the tide has turned and people have said no to the foreign, liberal elite (mainly Catholic countries) and embraced BREXIT.

We should use BREXIT as an example today and demonstrate on the field that we have had enough of foreign investors (the sinister Dermot Desmond and his evil cabal) and get tore into the tarriers. Fight fire with fire.

We made the dreadful mistake of employing a Portuguese manager who was not right for Rangers (sic) on a whole range of matters. As soon as he left, along with some of his Spanish/Mexican/Portuguese players and were replaced with Scottish/British players, we improved dramatically under Mr. Murty.

If we stop them this afternoon, they will implode with rage especially if we thwart their bid to record a new record of back to backs. So let us unsheathe the sword metaphorically speaking and put Timothy back in his box. Come on the Rangers (sic)![44]

Hilarious as this is, it's also pretty frightening to think that there are individuals walking among us that honestly believe this crap.

Also frightening, extremely disgusting and not in the least bit funny is the main way that The People channel their hatred.

It's only fairly recently that the sexual abuse of children has become a topic at all. For many years it was something that wasn't talked about. In the 60s, 70s and 80s, children were told not to talk to strangers; and that was it. Strangers, however, were not the problem. Most children suffered abuse at the hands of somebody they already knew. And, since it was something that everybody pretended that only strangers did, any child speaking up would find himself receiving a belt on the jaw for saying such bad things about his Uncle Charlie.

In Chapter 14 of my book, *Up to Our Knees*, I went into a lot of detail about the history of child abuse in the UK and how, now that there's far more of an appetite for investigation, a lot of people are looking for someone to blame. The old 'stranger' myth hasn't died out and fingers are constantly being pointed at 'the other'. For many, this has been, and still is, Catholics but Muslims are fast becoming the favourite scapegoat in the UK.

All over the world, it's been discovered that child abusers have wormed their way into any and every organisation involving children. The Summer Camp, an institution in America and France, has all but died out because of the revelations about child abuse going on there. The Boy Scouts, the Boys Brigade, schools, children's homes, sports clubs; all have been tainted due to the discovery of abusers in their midst. The latest scandal has been the uncovering of what might have been an organised gang of abusers in youth football.

There's no concrete evidence of this yet, but the discovery of more and more abusers would seem to suggest it. The English FA started an independent enquiry into the issue back in 2016.[45] This, obviously, can't be completed overnight; it's not just a case of finding out who the abusers were, it has to be discovered how they were able to infiltrate football clubs so that it can never happen again.

The SFA instituted the same kind of thing only a month later. 'It said the review would focus on "processes and procedures" in place both currently and historically in Scottish football.'[46] Of course, any allegations against individuals would be handed over to the police. It's not the football authorities' job to prosecute people in this respect; their remit is to ensure that football is, in future, a safe environment for children.

Sad to say, it seems as if very few football clubs, professional and amateur, have avoided being infiltrated by these perverts. Celtic and Rangers, being the biggest clubs in Scotland back in the day, were especially vulnerable. That, however, is something that The People don't understand; the clubs targeted by these individuals, or groups, were victims, not participants.

Whether you believe that Neo-Gers is a new club or, like The People, that it is 'still Rangers' is irrelevant in this respect. When historic child abuse was occurring, it was a different time, with different people involved. Nobody is going to point fingers at these folk for being duped, or for dealing with perverts in the same way that everybody else did back then. The People, though, can't accept this. In their minds, it was something that didn't happen at Ibrox and, if it did, everybody did the right thing and called the police.

In April 2017, a programme investigating historic child abuse in Scottish football was shown on BBC Scotland. The programme highlighted one Gordon Neely, who allegedly abused children at Hibs and Rangers, as well as at other clubs.[47] According to sources at Ibrox, Neely was sacked when an allegation was made, and the police were informed.[48] Police Scotland, however, were unable to confirm or deny that Rangers had made a complaint.[49]

The People seized on this police statement as somehow constituting proof that Rangers did indeed contact them.

> In that article he seems to make out that there is some doubt as to whether Rangers reported it to the police, it fails to say that the police cannot confirm or deny that a report was made and that's because of an on going investigation or they have no records of the report to confirm or deny, they can't say it didn't happen.[50]

Actually, it's not quite that simple. Apparently, 'it (the story of Neely being sacked from Rangers) is not connected to Police Scotland's current investigation into "non-recent" cases.'[51] There was also no evidence of a report being sent to the Procurator

Fiscal, which suggests that the police weren't informed after all. Nobody that was at Rangers at the time was willing to make any comment either.[52] A Neo-Gers spokesperson said, though, that 'All employees adhered to the strictest codes of conduct.'[53]

And therein lies the answer for all the secrecy, evasion and possible lies. Nobody wants to admit that folk at Rangers behaved exactly the same way as everybody else did back then. This has nothing to do with avoiding any finger-pointing; after all, it looks as if there are very few, if any, football clubs that would be in a position to do that. Everybody at Neo-Gers will be aware of this. The truth is that, rather than trying to avoid any finger-pointing by others, everyone connected with Rangers and Neo-Gers want to be the ones doing the finger-pointing. And that finger is only pointing at one, specific club.

There's no need to recount all the online comments, songs and chants about sexual abuse at Celtic Boys' Club; we're all familiar with them. If you remember, even Gordon Smith thought that a joke about the subject was worth a giggle.[54] So, it's not just The People that use child abuse in a disgusting, point-scoring way; those associated with both Ibrox clubs are quite prepared to do the same. They can hardly do this unless they keep up the pretence that such things never happened at Rangers and, if there was as much as a sniff of it, the police were contacted immediately.

Like all the other forms of hatred exhibited by The People, these desperate attempts to make out that only Celtic was affected by child abuse and even that an abuse ring operated at Celtic Park have become far more pronounced since Rangers died. Again, it's a symptom of the anger and culture of blame associated with The People. One commenter on *FollowFollow* summed up how they were feeling.

> We were made to beg for our licence, sign illegal agreements with the SFA the lot just to stay in the game and all because of one conman.
> What does covering up pedo's (sic) get you ? With 4 pedos (sic) (that we know of) within your club then there are no excuses.
> Scotland's real shame and still they are trying to cover it up.[55]

Of course, they couch all this bile in terms of wanting justice for the children that were abused. It is remarkably easy to show that this is not what they want at all. If they do want this, then why were they so desperate to denigrate Andy Muirhead when he urged all football fans in Scotland to stand together against child abuse to encourage victims to speak up?[56]

In May, what seemed, at first sight, a rather disturbing aspect of this whole business came to light.

> A former youth footballer who says he was sexually abused by a Rangers coach has been told by the club he should pursue his complaint with liquidators.
>
> The man claims he was abused within the Ibrox stadium by Gordon Neely who was head of youth development in the 1980s.
>
> But the alleged victim has been told by lawyers for Rangers (sic) that the duty of care is not with the current owners.
>
> They said that when the abuse took place Rangers were owned by a different company which was now in liquidation.[57]

To be honest, this looked worse than it was. Neo-Gers offered to help the man with counselling services and the advice to contact the liquidators was addressed to the man's solicitor, who was obviously seeking compensation for his client. The Neo-Gers lawyers were simply stating the truth, even though it was couched in terms of the continuity myth. The folk in charge nowadays can't be held liable for what happened nearly forty years ago. Celtic's lawyers would act in exactly the same way. Try telling that to The People, though.

> Quite a coincidence BBC Scotland trot this out as we await the verdict on the Paedo ring at the piggery. Getting their retaliation in first, anyone?[58]

> Perfect timing for this story to be released so the "aye butters" can have a deflection tactic when the shit hits the fan at their sordid club.[59]

69

Doubts were even cast on whether the story was true or not.

> I don't know, maybe it's just me but this story feels
> wrong somehow. I know we employed this paedo
> creep thanks to the Leith tarriers not warning anyone
> he was a nonce but was this "David" even on our
> books? Did this actually happen?
> The one thing I don't understand is why the fuck he
> would have a season ticket after that.
> No the thing stinks in my opinion.[60]

One, lone voice of reason stood out among the bile and
bigotry.

> Horrific if true.
> Let's not play whataboutery.
> Police informed, check.
> Now let's ensure this and every instance at every club
> are probed fully and the findings of police
> investigations about the bastards who commit such
> acts and the worse bastards and scum at clubs who
> concealed or facilitated such acts are highlighted. And
> hammered.
> If anyone at Rangers was guilty they deserve punished.
> As do Rangers if they didn't report it, retained the
> abuser in employment, or paid off victims / families
> and allowed such conduct to continue.
> Let's get this all out there rather than be Scotland's
> shame. For every club in Scotland. Every detail whilst
> protecting the identity of the complainer.[61]

Now, nobody could argue against that, but nobody among The
People was interested. In fact, all they wanted was to be able to
take the moral high ground.

> Whoever penned that statement for Rangers (sic)
> should be shown the door. It is terrible PR to be in
> any way defensive in such matters and missed an open
> goal to take the higher ground and call for a full open

investigation of the conduct of all clubs in dealing with child abuse claims.[62]

There was also not much in the way of sympathy for the victim.

> If 'David', Rangers fan, and season ticket holder at Ibrox, is so concerned about justice- why is he pursuing us for monetary gain when he knows our recent financial situation?[63]

The whole, disgusting attitude of The People toward child sexual abuse was laid bare in the reaction of one of their number to a story about a Celtic-supporting member of the SFA Board. The man had said something mildly derogatory about The People back in 2006. (See Chapter 13.) In among the howls of protests and demands for the man's resignation, one Neo-Gers supporter had this to say:

> Hopefully they've found out he was fiddling with Yong (sic) boys.[64]

Now, that spoke volumes about The People.

It looked as if, no matter what happened, The People weren't prepared to budge an inch on their insistence that child sexual abuse was a 'Celtic thing' and a 'Catholic thing'. Of course, the only basis for this was sheer bigotry; a bigotry that can be summed up in this little statement:

> I'm so glad I get up in the morning and look at my big handsome Protestant mug in the mirror & thank my lucky fucking stars I ain't one of those despicable job dodging, wean touching, bead rattling, benefit claiming, giro cashing, tarmac laying, lawnmower sharpening, caravan dwelling, pikey cunts!!!!!!![65]

71

7
A Different Kind of Tension

Everybody knows the story of Pandora's Box. What most folk aren't aware of, however, is that, in ancient Greece, there were two versions of the story. We're all familiar with Hope being at the bottom of the box and Pandora releasing her to make up for all the evils she'd let loose on the world. In the alternative version, though, Hope wasn't a goodie; in fact, she was considered the worst thing in the box. Hope draws people on to failure after failure, disaster after disaster, giving them the false feeling that everything's going to turn out alright in the end. It is this version of Hope that seems more realistic when one considers The People.

Sometimes you almost feel sorry for The People; no matter how many times they get beaten down, they're soon back up again, waiting for the next blow. There's nothing positive about this ability for resurgence; in fact, it only serves to make them even more bitter. Every time they're due to face Celtic, the triumph of hope over experience makes them believe that they're going to win. So arrogant are they that they refuse to be budged from this belief until it's too late.

This time, they were facing Celtic at Hampden in the semi-final of the Scottish Cup. Apparently, the Neo-Gers players cheered in the changing-room when they heard that they'd drawn Celtic.[1] Rumour has it that The People cheered as well. This was before the 3-2 defeat at Ibrox, though, so perhaps we can forgive their delusion.

Even after Celtic had beaten them, that arrogant belief still lingered. The ned's ned, Barry Ferguson, was in the Daily Record a few days later to tell us all that Celtic had only won through sheer luck! According to him, Neo-Gers were the better team, but the gods were smiling on Brendan Rodgers.[2] As everyone was quick to point out to His Thickness, the only lucky ones were Neo-Gers themselves, who had benefited from mistakes by Boyata. He wasn't listening, though, and continued to hold onto this ridiculous position.[3]

Meanwhile, results since that defeat to Celtic appeared to point to Neo-Gers having a chance this time; as far as The People were concerned at any rate. After losing 1-0 to Kilmarnock, Neo-Gers rallied somewhat to draw 2-2 against Motherwell at Fir Park. Celtic had played at the same venue nearly two weeks before; a game that ended in a miserable 0-0 draw.

Celtic's next match was against Dundee in a midweek game at Celtic Park, again resulting in a scoreless draw. Three days later, Neo-Gers exhibited what the BBC called 'a dominant display' to beat Dundee 4-0 at Ibrox.[4] Surely that meant Neo-Gers was a better team than Celtic?[5] It was the kind of logic one has come to expect from The People and, yet again, they were going into a match against Celtic full of confidence.

The players seemed to be confident as well, with Alfredo Morelos already on record as promising his family that he was definitely going to score against Celtic at Hampden.[6] Others, too, were keen to get involved, including, most likely, Kreosote Kenny, who had scored the opener against Dundee and whom Keith Jackson stated would have to be a must-start against Celtic.[7]

Strangely, the only one that wasn't building up Neo-Gers' chances was Honest Dave. In what was supposed to be a rousing appeal to The People to buy season tickets, he claimed that a new manager would soon be forthcoming; one that would guarantee immediate success. Not surprisingly, everybody saw this as a statement that Murty would no longer be in charge next season. It was hardly a vote of confidence with the semi-final coming up.[8]

This, however, didn't seem to dent the confidence of The People, the players and the agnivores. Maybe they should have read what Neil Cameron had said about the game against Dundee in the *Herald*.

'THE scoreboard never lies but this was an occasion when it felt as if it told a half-truth. It did not feel like a 4-0 game.

For long spells, the Rangers performance was so ugly that it could have been dreamt up by Victor Hugo. If they play in this manner against Celtic next week in the Scottish Cup semi-final, their biggest game of the season, they will get battered at Hampden.'[9]

Then again, even if they had read this article, The People would no doubt dismiss it as the work of a 'Raynjurz-Hatur' or even a

'Prodissint-Hatur'. Pointing out the truth to The People is always equivalent to the story of *Cassandra*; cursed with the power to tell the future but not be believed by anyone.

For those prepared to look, there were signs that all was not as it should be at Ibrox. The twenty-one-year-old David Bates had been praised to the heavens ever since he came on as a substitute, replacing Bruno Alves, at Celtic Park on December 30th. He was awarded Man of the Match for his display in that game.[10] After that, even when Alves was fit again, Murty preferred young Master Bates, saying,

> We brought him on against Celtic before new year because we trust him, because we understand the improvements he has made.
> Is he the finished article? No, not yet. But he is doing things I like and things are getting better.
> He needs to see from me a degree of trust and respect for what he has done.[11]

Unfortunately, that 'trust and respect' didn't extend to a decent remuneration for what Master Bates was doing. His contract was up in the summer and, of course, his agent was looking out for his interests, as he's supposed to do. Apparently, he and his agent asked Neo-Gers for a pay rise, which was turned down, so he signed with Hamburg on a four-year contract, starting in the summer.[12]

The agnivores rounded on Bates immediately, pointing out that

> His package would have outstripped considerably the salary levels of other young Rangers and Ibrox chairman Dave King and his board decided to draw the line on a player who has made just 19 appearances for the club.[13]

That must have stuck in Bates's craw a bit, considering that he was first-choice defender over Bruno Alves, who, apparently, was on €38,000 a week,[14] which is over £33,000. The fact that Bates had asked for £7,500 a week perhaps shows what his club *really* thought of him.

It's worth remembering Phil Mac Giolla Bhain's tales about the split in the team while Boxy was there.[15] The team was divided into two camps: Boxy's duds in one camp, everybody else in the other. It's hard to imagine that these two mutually antipathetic groups would suddenly become the best of pals just because Boxy had gone. It's also hard to imagine that what Phil Mac Giolla Bhain called the 'Quintessentially British WhatsApp Group' would be too chuffed about Bates being knocked back while Alves kept coining it in. And, let's face it, Alves had turned out to be as much use as a chocolate teapot, or a tifo organised by the *Union Bears*. There could be trouble ahead.

Murty appeared to have chosen a side when he castigated Bates for taking the mercenary option.

> So take emotion out of the situation, take the fact he is a Rangers (sic) supporter out of the situation, there is a load of money on the table. Extrapolate out of that what you will.[16]

The only thing that you could possibly extrapolate from that, and the rest of what Murty had to say, was that Bates was a greedy, little bastard. Luckily for both Murty and Bates, the defender was out injured so there would be no difficulties over whether he would be chosen to appear at Hampden or not. It left Murty clear to play Alves, albeit as a substitute, without any hint of bad blood between Bates and his manager.

Meanwhile, the football authorities were faced with a dilemma. When Celtic beat Hamilton 2-1 on the 8th of April, it meant that they only needed one more win to secure the league title.[17] There were five games left to play, with the 'split' meaning that all the top-six teams had to face each other one more time. The big worry was that Celtic were due to face Neo-Gers at home; would The People be able to face Celtic winning the title against their team?

Police Scotland weren't too keen on the idea either, conjuring up visions of 1999.[18] It's a match that the agnivores love to hark back to, as if there had been a huge riot or something. Strangely, it's always made out as if whoever threw that coin just hated to see Rangers winning; no mention of Hugh Dallas and his blatant cheating. And yet, Neo-Gers supporters rioting and beating folk up at Hampden in 2016 is painted as them 'protecting their players'.

The People were also responsible for the riot at Hampden in 1980. Even though it's evident that this is true, even from accounts given decades after the event,[19] nobody will come straight out and admit it. The People don't like getting beat; especially if the defeat means their opponents have won a cup or such like.

Of course, The People couldn't wait to point the finger at the Celtic supporters; yet again, bringing up 1999. Brendan Rodgers had said that the whole business of trying to stop Celtic winning the title against Neo-Gers was a 'sad indictment' of Scotland.[20] One Neo-Gers supporting halfwit had an answer to this ready:

> Rodgers says it is a sad indictment of our society. Then what does it say about our society when the champions hum and haw over wearing a poppy and choose to play the Republic of Ireland to play in their captain's testimonial? It's double standards.[21]

Quite apart from making no sense, all that little tirade served to show was how bigoted The People were. Maybe the authorities were right to avoid Celtic winning the title against Neo-Gers; who could tell how The People might react this time.

The SPFL released the fixtures list on the 11th of April.[22] Celtic were drawn to face Hibs at Easter Road in their first post-split encounter. That would be on the 21st of April, with Neo-Gers visiting Celtic Park eight days later. Surely Celtic could be relied upon to wrap up the title against Neil Lennon's men? In the meantime, there was that semi-final to take care of.

If anyone expected surprises in the Neo-Gers line-up at Hampden, they were to be sorely disappointed. Even though Kreosote Kenny had supposedly impressed in his return to the team against Dundee, his only reward was to be on the bench at Hampden. Just like The People, Murty seemed to put his trust in hope rather than experience and, yet again, Morelos was going to play up front.

In big games throughout the world, opposing managers are apt to play mind games with each other, seeking to gain some kind of upper hand. It doesn't quite work like that in Scotland; it's the media that play the mind games and this time was no exception. The Daily Record is the main culprit for this and they had the headline: 'Graeme Murty challenges Rangers (sic) stars to win Scottish Cup'. The man himself said, referring to the 3-2 defeat,

> We should remember how much it hurt, remember we had good opportunities to get something from the game and I want them to use that as fuel to drive them to a more positive day.[23]

Maybe he could take something positive from the treatment the Record doled out to Brendan Rodgers. *His* headline said, 'Celtic boss Brendan Rodgers reveals fear of failure against Rangers (sic) is what drives him on'.[24] Actually, in the article, Rodgers said absolutely nothing about fear, merely pointing out that he takes one game at a time. No doubt Murty put this up on the changing-room wall at Hampden to inspire the troops.

His team could have done with some inspiration because they were no match for Celtic. The BBC report said that Neo-Gers were 'brutally ripped apart'[25] and, really, there's no other way to describe the match. Right from the start, Celtic dominated, leaving the Neo-Gers players more and more flustered and frustrated. Celtic were two up at half-time and could easily have scored more if they hadn't wasted some opportunities in front of goal. Neo-Gers were all over the place, while The People could only watch in horror. There wasn't a peep out of them for practically the whole match.

Frustrated players make mistakes, and nobody was making more than Andy Halliday. Not only was he losing out in tackles and giving the ball away, but his temper was beginning to get the better of him and he had started to lash out a bit. The way he was going, it wouldn't be too long before he was sent off. Starting the second half with only ten men would have been a nightmare so, quite rightly, Murty replaced Halliday with Windass, even though there were only a few minutes until half-time.

To say that Halliday wasn't happy about being substituted would be an understatement and he expressed his displeasure quite vocally. For some strange reason, the Daily Record reported this tirade as being directed toward a supporter[26] when everyone could see that he was shouting at the bench. It wasn't clear at whom he was yelling but the likelihood was that it was the manager.

The second half was no better for Neo-Gers, even though Celtic took their foot off the pedal. Nobody could, and nobody did, complain about the two penalties (yes, two!) that Celtic were awarded. And what made those two penalties even stranger was that it was Brother Boaby Madden that was the referee. Yes, you read that right. One of the penalties he gave was the same as the one he refused last year, when Clint Hill clattered Leigh Griffiths.[27] No doubt Madden suffered for those decisions down the lodge.

The first penalty was given when Ross McCrorie pulled down Moussa Dembélé in the box. Madden had no other option but to send McCrorie off, meaning that Murty had to quickly rearrange his team. Another defender was needed, so off came Candeias, and on went Alves. Candeias, however, just like Halliday, seemed to take umbrage at being replaced, as if it was something personal. He stormed down the tunnel in a massive huff.

Most of The People had left long before the final whistle, so the Neo-Gers team was able to leave the pitch without suffering the customary boos. Anybody with eyes, though, could see that they were practically booing each other. When they left the field of play, they didn't leave together, consoling one another for the defeat. Instead, they walked off in little groups, as if they didn't want to be associated with the bastards in the other groups. Blame hung over the whole scene like a bad smell.

Almost as soon as the match was over, Kreosote Kenny's wife was straight onto Twitter to complain about her man being left on the bench. She said, 'Fact kenny is a big game old firm (sic) player' and added 'N btw he's fitter than any1 I've ever met.'[28] Obviously, things weren't going too well at Ibrox and, as it turned out, we hadn't heard the half of it yet.

As the players left the pitch, there was more going on than first appeared. Apparently, Greg Docherty and Alfredo Morelos started arguing almost as soon as the final whistle blew, while Bruno Alves, of all people, tried to calm them down. The fight continued, and the pair came to blows in the tunnel, having to be pulled apart by their teammates. Then, as the Daily Record put it, 'It's understood there were more heated exchanges inside the Rangers dressing room as tempers boiled over after a humiliating defeat to the champions.'[29]

It didn't take too long to find out who was involved in those 'heated exchanges'. Kreosote Kenny and Lee 'Captain Beaky' Wallace had a serious go at Murty in the changing room. As the Daily Record said,

Miller and Wallace let loose with a savage verbal onslaught that slaughtered his (Murty's) pre-match planning and matchday preparation in front of stunned team-mates in the dressing room after the 4-0 defeat.[30]

Whether there was any violence involved isn't clear, but KK's and Captain Beaky's behaviour was bad enough to warrant them both being suspended by the Ibrox board. KK's contract was up in the summer but Captain Beaky still had twelve months on his. Apparently, though, he was going to be 'made available for transfer in the summer',[31] so his arse was out the window as well. A Neo-Gers source said that 'certain individuals had been a "disruptive influence" at Ibrox for too long.'[32] It looked as if Phil Mac Giolla Bhain had been right.

The People might sympathise with KK and CB, but they were of the opinion that discipline must be maintained.[33] The agnivores felt the same and ex-players were wheeled out to back up this stance.[34] Not everyone, however, was singing from the same Orange Order song sheet. It looked as if Jabba was losing his touch.

Keith 'Jet' Jackson was the first to step out of line, saying that the board was wrong to get rid of KK and CB; in his opinion, it was Murty that should have been fired.

Given Murty is already a busted flush in the eyes of his own disenfranchised squad, surely it would have made more sense to let Wallace and Miller attempt to bring this group back together for the final five games of a season which could now become even more of an embarrassment than it already is.

The risk here appears obvious to everyone outside of King's beleaguered regime. These players were already in a mutinous mood with Murty and now there is even less reason for them to fall into line behind a manager who has used up the last of their respect by emptying two of their most valued team-mates.[35]

Now, Jackson happens to be the Chief Sports Writer at the Daily Record, which means that he's in charge. One wonders how he'd feel if one of his subordinates kept handing in stories in which the Big

Lie was ignored and the truth was told about Rangers' death. Imagine things then got to the point where said writer then shouted at Jackson, in front of everyone, telling him how useless he was. Would Jackson throw him the keys to his office and tell him to take over? Would he hell!

You'll notice that Jackson makes a big deal over how the players would now lose all respect for Murty; but what respect would they have if he just caved in? Jackson continues,

> Word has it Miller and Wallace were spotted late at night in the team hotel before Sunday's mismatch, locked in a stony-faced conversation about Murty's tactical plan. It looked very much to those who witnessed this conversation as if they had unlocked some serious flaws in Murty's orders. If so, they were hardly wrong.[36]

If this pair thought there were going to be problems with Murty's tactics, then why didn't they mention it to him *before* the match? The fact that they didn't suggests that they actually wanted their team to lose and couldn't wait to rub Murty's face in it. Just like under Boxy, it was a war for control between the manager and a gang of troublemakers. In Jackson's opinion, the troublemakers should have won.

Others lined up to take the side of Kreosote Kenny and Captain Beaky, including Lee McCulloch[37] and Barry Ferguson,[38] who compared what was happening to his own situation when he was accused of undermining Paul Le Guen. Apparently, he did no such thing and wasn't prepared to believe that KK and CB had done so either. (Aye, we believe you, Barry!) Even John Hartson was dragged into it, saying, in a rambling monologue, 'Listen, it could be a case of Rangers (sic) taking the easy way out, they've got a bit of a history of sacking players. They sacked their legend Barry Ferguson.'[39]

It was beginning to look as if it wasn't Keith Jackson that had stepped out of line; it was everybody else. As the days wore on, it was becoming clear that the Level 5 line was 'Miller and Wallace good; Murty bad.' Also, it seemed, players were rallying round KK and CB, telling a different story from the one we'd heard. 'And a significant number of players are now willing to give testimony, adamant that there was no 'bust-up' between manager Murty and the two accused.'[40] No prizes for guessing who made up that 'significant number'.

It was easy to turn around and blame King for everything that had happened; after all, he'd undermined Murty with his talk of a new, and better, manager. In this way of looking at things, the players had lost any respect they still had for Murty. He'd set out his plans, name his team etc. only for the players to turn round and say, like the boy in the Wyclef Jean Virgin Mobile advert,[41] 'You ain't my real manager!' And, then, a head would appear and say, 'Oh, Graeme, honey! Davy needs love!'

A week after the drubbing at Hampden, Neo-Gers beat a shambolic Hearts 2-1 at Ibrox. Daniel Candeias scored Neo-Gers' second and ran to the dugout to celebrate. He ran right past his manager to hug Andy Halliday and, then, other players joined in.[42] This was tantamount to a snub to Graeme Murty and, on the surface at least, substantiates the story about the whole team having no respect for their manager due to King's blunder. There was, however, a lot more to it than that.

As we saw earlier, there were those in the team that were squarely behind Kreosote Kenny and Captain Beaky. Not only were they saying that there was no 'bust up' but they were prepared to swear on a stack of Bibles that Murty hadn't even been in the changing room at the time.[43] You can't buy that kind of loyalty!

As many folk are fond of pointing out, Phil Mac Giolla Bhain isn't right all the time; but it looks as if he was certainly right about Kreosote Kenny and his clique. Two managers in a row had had to put up with this nonsense and, if King was serious about bringing in another manager, it had to be nipped in the bud. There should only be one boss in the changing room.

8
Why Can't I Touch It?

If you've read Joseph Heller's book, you'll know what *Catch 22* means. The pilots in the book had no way out of flying missions constantly. With no leave available, the only possible way out was for medical reasons. If you could prove you were crazy, then you could get leave on medical grounds. That, however, was easier said than done. It didn't matter what you did; the very fact that you wanted out of flying proved you were sane. In fact, the only way to prove you were a lunatic was to volunteer for more missions. Of course, once you'd volunteered, you were duty-bound to go on the missions. It was the perfect trap.

Neo-Gers has been stuck with its own version of *Catch 22* for a while now. The team badly needs investment if they're ever going to catch up with Celtic. It's been said time and again that the best source of revenue would be to compete in Europe. The big bucks, however, aren't really available in the Europa League; participation in the Champions League would be needed to make any serious cash. To get into that illustrious competition, however, Neo-Gers would have to win the league. So, to get the money required to overtake Celtic Neo-Gers need to…er…overtake Celtic. It's hardly an ideal situation.

Of course, there are other ways for a football club to make money and The People have come up with some outlandish ideas. How about a premium-rate phone number, with Neo-Gers supporters calling in 'from all over the world' to get the 'honest truth' read by 'club legends'? Or doing a fundraiser for Poppy Scotland, where the money's split between neo-Gers and the charity? And then there could be Amy McDonald, doing a fundraising gig for free.[1]

Stadium tours have always been a popular suggestion, especially when teams came to play Celtic. As they usually did, Neo-Gers offered any opposition that Celtic faced the use of the training facilities at Murry Park. (Oops! Sorry. Auchenhowie.) Some bright sparks suggested offering tours of Ibrox to visiting supporters, so they could 'see some history and class'. One enterprising soul came up with the idea of offering a reduction to the entrance fee if the customer was wearing the top of Celtic's opponents.[2]

Another one of The People had an even better brainwave. Why not have a fly-on-the-wall documentary series about the day-to-day operations at Ibrox, particularly focusing on Director of Football, Mark Allen? A big name (he suggested Karl Pilkington) and a bit of a comedic element would broaden the appeal of the show; Netflix would snap it up![3]

I don't have a reference but who can forget the idea suggested by one fantasist of lining cars along the sidelines at Ibrox? Spectators would pay to sit in the cars to watch the match; the more expensive the car, the more you'd pay. He even envisaged a tank taking its place in the vehicular ranks. Presumably, the disabled, who usually sit near the sidelines, would just be told to piss off.

The best one, though, has to be the 'T in the Park' idea; a sort of 'Williams in Wellies'. This would showcase the best of 'Scottish Protestant culture'. As the man with the plan put it, 'Our culture has plenty of musicians from flute and pipe bands to crooners singing Penny Arcade and old Rangers songs.'[4] Millions, apparently, would be ready to part with their hard-earned to live in a tent or caravan and be up to their knees in mud, instead of blood, for a whole weekend. It could even become an annual event and make Neo-Gers 'one of the richest clubs in the world!'[5]

What might be termed a trial run for this kind of 'Gathering of the Klans' was held in a Glasgow hotel on the 31st of March. It was called 'Rangers 9 In a Row 20th Anniversary Dinner' and folk paid £70 per skull to meet and eat with former players. It was a bit of a misnomer since the final title win of that nine-in-a-row came in 1997; obviously counting is not a strong point at Ibrox. The night turned into a bigot-fest with anti-Catholic songs to the fore. The police had to be called in when things turned violent and there was an assault.[6] No doubt 'Bigots in the Park' would turn out the same.

The website *Ibrox Noise* came up with its own 'ten-part plan' to 'rebuild' Neo-Gers.[7] This involved spending money (doesn't it always) on decent players, especially defenders. *Ibrox Noise*, unlike others, were able to say where the money was to come from for these players. Unfortunately, they were pinning all their hopes on Morelos being sold for several millions. Anyone, however, with a

83

reasonable level of intelligence knew that all the shite about Chinese clubs chasing Morelos was just that: shite. They'd have to do better than that.

Their big money-making idea was for Neo-Gers to secure some kind of TV rights deal in an Asian country, such as Indonesia. Why they think folk in Asia would possibly be interested in watching Neo-Gers they don't day. It's not as if they have any Asian players, so they've not exactly got a selling point. And if they were to sign any, they'd have to be cheap and would probably end up on the bench or not playing at all. Yep; that would soon rope in the punters!

If all the promises made to The People by the agnivores had come to fruition, of course, none of these nonsensical dreams would have been necessary. Certainly, The People had chased off a real billionaire just to get Real Rangers Men in the Blue Room, but they'd been told they were getting a *rich* Real Rangers Man in the shape of Honest Dave King. Well, King *was* rich but, when it came to Neo-Gers, he had short arms and deep pockets.

King and his board might not have paid a lot of attention to the mad, money-making schemes of The People, but they had to come up with some of their own. The most controversial of these plans came at the end of March, when Stewart Robertson, the Neo-Gers Managing Director, announced, 'We are delighted to welcome Vaporized to our portfolio of partners and sponsors.'[8]

This, however, was no mere sponsorship, with a prominent advertising space at the side of the pitch; *Vaporized* was to 'become the official vaping partner' of Neo-Gers, no less. What that meant was that *Vaporized* was going to be opening a store within Ibrox and that fish-ell Neo-Gers e-liquids would be launched. Vaping would also be permitted on the Ibrox concourses.[9]

A lot of people think that vaping is a way of giving up smoking altogether, but that's not how it's marketed. The companies that make and sell the products make no mention of them being like nicotine chewing-gum and the like. Instead, it's a different way of taking nicotine; it's a replacement for cigarettes, not a way of giving them up. Health professionals are undecided about the long-term effects, but all agree that they're a safer alternative to cigarettes.[10]

Alcohol sponsorship in sports has been a controversial topic for decades now. Other countries ban it completely and there have been arguments galore about it in Parliament. Does it encourage more drinking? Well, the producers of alcoholic beverages wouldn't do it otherwise, would they? There's also a debate that it encourages underage drinking, since alcohol is being associated with 'manly' pursuits like football and rugby. Although there is no ban in place, it's certainly noticeable that there is a lot less alcohol sponsorship in football than there used to be. It seems as if football clubs are self-policing in this respect.

Whatever the arguments about alcohol sponsorship, there is no such debate when it comes to smoking. You won't see any football teams with 'Marlboro' or 'Rothmans' on their strips. And this is where the Neo-Gers 'partnership' with *Vaporized* runs up against problems. When cigarette advertising was facing a ban, the argument of the tobacco companies was that it was just targeting people that were already smokers, trying to persuade them to change brands. Nobody, however, believed a word of it and reckoned that the real targets of cigarette advertising were the young and that the tobacco companies were looking for a new generation of smokers.

No matter how much safer than smoking vaping is, most health professionals would agree that it's not the kind of thing that non-smokers should take up.[11] Even vaping manufacturers agree on this and even admit that vaping by non-smokers could actually lead to them smoking cigarettes.[12] In this respect, is it really a product that a football club should be associated with?

Even some of The People weren't too happy about it and didn't want folk at Ibrox blowing their vaping smoke, steam or whatever it is, next to them.

> Sitting next to some c unt (sic) who thinks it's going to be okay to blow a plume of smoke in your direction. Nice one Rangers (sic)![13]

> Fag smoke smells better than those f()cking things. Give me the boak.[14]

> We're scraping the barrel.[15]

Most of The People, however, won't be in the least concerned about the possible health effects of vaping; they'll be putting the e-cigarettes and bottles of liquid to a quite different use. Why go to the trouble of smuggling in batteries and golf balls when you can stock up on missiles, quite legally, at half-time?

Vaporized held a competition to suggest names for their Ibrox-themed liquids. The winners, who were paraded on the company's website,[16] were 'treated' to a day in the Hospitality Suite at Ibrox to watch the Neo-Gers v Kilmarnock game. Considering how dire that match was, it seemed more of a punishment. The website admitted that some suggestions 'just weren't safe for the public domain';[17] you can imagine what some of those were like, full of references to the Pope, Ireland and even child abuse.

The ones chosen as the winners were necessarily bland: *Tobacco the Net, Ibrox Ice, Simply the Zest, Strawbarry Ferguson, Peach of a Goal* and *Boys in Blue Razz*. It's hard to read any of them without groaning out loud. Some of the ones suggested by Celtic supporters, such as *Liquid8* and *Morelos Mist*,[18] were much better, though unlikely to be used. I'm sure the reader has some more appropriate suggestions!

Meanwhile, although Neo-Gers had, apparently, severed all ties with Mike Ashley, they were still stuck with Puma as their strip manufacturer; to the end of the season, at any rate. This meant that Neo-Gers were obligated to carry adverts for Puma, even on their Twitter account. One such advert caused uproar among The People, since it was for a new range of – gasp! – green boots![19]

According to Phil Mac Giolla Bhain, the denizens of the Blue Room had tried to avoid this embarrassment by asking Puma not to run the advert. There was no telling Puma, though, and the company just ran roughshod over the concerns of the Ibrox board.[20] There is, however, another possibility.

Although The People were angry at their club, it's pretty obvious that most of their ire would be directed toward Puma. After all, wasn't the German company part-and-parcel of the whole Charles Green 'onerous contracts' bit? No doubt, many of The People were desperate for the day when Neo-Gers had a completely different supplier.

It was only a couple of weeks later that Neo-Gers announced that they had a new supplier for the new season: *Hummel*. According to the Daily Record, the Danish company was chosen from 'more than 10 offers received by kit suppliers'.[21] That begs the question: if Neo-Gers had chosen *Hummel*, which isn't exactly a top brand, then who the hell were the others that they knocked back? It's more likely the case that *Hummel* was the only company willing to do business with the Ibrox club and the agnivores were spinning things as usual.

The *Hummel* website shows that the company and Neo-Gers were practically made for each other. Among various blurbs is the following:

> Our sponsorships focus on uniqueness. Unique culture, values and individuals daring to break conventions in order to reach their goals.[22]

Well, that was all certainly true of Neo-Gers. The People revel in their 'culture', which, uniquely, isn't a culture at all but simply a hatred of everyone that's different from them. And as for breaking conventions, Neo-Gers has emulated its predecessor at Ibrox by spending money it doesn't have and relying on handshakes at the SFA to get it through. The blurb goes on:

> We also look for the underdogs - those who rarely win, but where the soul, legacy and dreams are sometimes even bigger.[23]

That sums up Neo-Gers succinctly; a new club, often struggling, but with a high self-opinion and ideas way above its station. The People certainly wouldn't like that particular description.

That's where that Puma advert came in useful. Who would want a big company bossing the club around? Far better to be sponsored and supplied by a smaller company; one that seems to be grateful for the opportunity. As the *Hummel* CEO put it,

> We are extremely proud to have been chosen as the new technical partner to one of the world's oldest and most famous football clubs. Words can barely describe the level of excitement at our head office this morning when we announced this fantastic new partnership to our International staff.[24]

Now, that's the kind of sycophantic utterance The People like to hear. With arse-licking of that quality, it seemed highly unlikely that *Hummel* would ever dare put green boots on any Neo-Gers social media.

A new kit supplier is one thing, but a retail outlet is essential if any money is to be made from replica kits. If you go onto the *Rangers (sic) Megastore* website it has a section, as all retail sites have, where you can contact the headquarters with complaints etc. There are two options: you can contact them by post or e-mail. The postal address is:

Rangers Megastore
Unit A, Brook Park East,
Meadow Lane,
Shirebrook.
NG20 8RY.

If that particular address doesn't ring any bells, then here's the e-mail address: Customer Services (cs@sportsdirect.com).[25] Get it now? Obviously, Mike Ashley is still running the show when it comes to the retail side of Neo-Gers.

It's something that The People and the agnivores haven't looked into, choosing to believe the story of how Neo-Gers was now getting the lion's share of retail profits. They ignored the fact that Neo-Gers was no longer involved in the retail side at all; Rangers (sic) Retail had been wound up. All they had was a deal with Sports Direct, which, apparently, still owned and operated the Megastore. The feel-good story when the deal was struck was:

(Neo-Gers) will now receive by far the majority of *net* profits from the retail operations at the Megastore and Webstore together with an equal share of all *net* profits from sales through SD.[26] (My italics.)

That word *net* made all the difference to how the deal operated. Sports Direct would be subtracting all its operating expenses, storage, delivery etc. before handing over any cash. The new kit deal with *Hummel*, then, wouldn't bring any more money to Neo-Gers; Ashley's company would still be the main beneficiary.

As early as January, well before the *Hummel* deal was announced, some of The People expressed concern about retailing. A deal with *Argos* was suggested, which, among a good deal of derision, seemed like a good idea to some.[27] There were those that liked the idea of a different retail outlet and came up with *Asda*, among others. None of them, however, suggested closing the Megastore and its associated website, meaning that they weren't quite as clever as they thought.

Unlike these dreamers, nobody at Neo-Gers had even hinted at any kind of new retail outlet. Not that they wouldn't want to seek a new retail deal; the probability was that they couldn't. Ashley still had them firmly by the bollocks.

By May, problems were already coming to the fore. There was no need to worry about the Neo-Gers players turning up in old strips for their Euro qualifiers as, apparently, the team kits were going to be ready in time. Unfortunately, though, Billy 'Burger' King and his family wouldn't be able to get their hands on replicas until later; possibly much later.

The Neo-Gers Supporters Liaison Officer, Greg Marshall explained the situation in a reply to a tweet.

> Peter, the previous regimes signed the retails/kit deals which have influenced the timings for the upcoming season still. The club have done as well as could be hoped in regards to this issue. From 2019/20 there should be no residual influence.[28]

Now, that sounded ominous. It looked as if The People wouldn't be able to hide their considerable bulks under XXXXXXXXL tops when they were on holiday. Indeed, things were probably even worse than that. Greg Marshall had another tweet, saying, 'To be clear the kits will be out well before Christmas…'[29] His other tweets saying that things would be normalised in 2019, however, had The People worried.

> If a club or manufacturer are incapable of unveiling a new kit launch during the summer (the absolute peak time, with everyone excited about the new season, new players, new manager, new hopes and in holiday mode with kids off for the summer) then something is seriously wrong. It's like releasing Christmas decorations in May!

Obviously I don't know what is or isn't happening or what may happen, and sometimes things can occur outwith your control but if we don't release a new kit until Christmas we will lose out on significant monies.[30]

Good old Greg explained what was causing the delay. 'Our contact with Puma has not ended yet.'[31] There was no indication, though, of when it was going to end. It seemed to some of The People that they had been taken for mugs yet again. This was especially true given the identity of the Supporters' Liaison Officer. Greg Marshall, it so happened, was the manager of the Louden Tavern and son of the owner. Both had featured in *daviesleftpeg*'s 'Tales of Spivery'.[32]

The folk moaning about the delay in the release of replica kits were also worried about how those kits would be retailed.

They have no retail distribution deal in place yet. Can't even start negotiations until end of July. No supply deals for IP carrying product can commence until then either because whatever distributor is chosen will have a say in what licensed products they sell and who makes it.[33]

The problem is they don't have a retail partner to handle the development and logistics supply of all licensed products and anticipate it will be early August before a deal is done. The last thing they want is to have to announce a new deal with SD.[34]

These guys had hit the nail squarely on the head. *Hummel* could churn out as many replica kits as they liked but, with nobody to sell them, they'd simply be causing a clutter. For all the talk of retail partners, it seemed that The People still didn't understand the reality of the situation.

Fuck SD, what would be so difficult to sell them at the Megastore and Online only[35]

As we have already seen, Sports Direct still owns the Megastore, as well as 100% of the Rangers (sic) Retail company, which includes online sales. The only way that Neo-Gers were going to benefit from kit sales would be if The People bought them online, straight from *Hummel*. The only other way would be for the board to set up a barra on Paisley Road West. 'Erzi fish-ell Raynjurz strip – three furra tenner!'

Those elements of The People that were desperate to see wee Billy in a Neo-Gers top, following behind the Walk in July, were treated to some good news near the end of May. Somebody had discovered a shop in the Turkish holiday resort of Marmaris selling an orange Neo-Gers top, with *Hummel* chevrons and everything.[36] Since Mehmet's Boutique seemed to have a plentiful supply of these illicit shirts, it would only be a matter of time before they appeared at *The Barras* and other markets in Scotland. No doubt these tops would practically disintegrate on first contact with water and Persil, but that wouldn't unduly concern the 'Great Unwashed', would it?

9
Paradise

The SPFL mandarins' cunning plan ended up being a failure. Celtic went to Easter Road on the 21st of April expecting a title party at the end of the match. Instead, Hibs won 2-1 in a hard-fought game, where Neil Lennon's team were determined to come out on top.[1] It meant that Celtic would have to wait at least another weak to be crowned Champions. Neo-Gers were coming to Celtic Park on the 29th – the scenario the authorities had been determined to avoid. The Celtic Park toilets braced themselves.

Of course, the more paranoid among The People were convinced that Celtic had lain down to Hibs. Since Rangers had always relied on dodgy officials and there had been suspicions of the odd fix, for example, against Dunfermline in 2003,[2] The People assume that everybody else behaves the same way. And the fixes still go on, with the heated balls guaranteeing Neo-Gers home games in the Scottish Cup when they have to face top-tier opposition. To The People, though, none of this happened or happens; it's everyone else that are the cheats. Some of them even believe they were cheated out of the Scottish Cup in 2016![3]

The Hibs v Celtic game had some of them absolutely incensed. The phones at the Daily Record Hotline were red-hot as the People called in to vent their spleens.

> It was blatant move by Brendan Rodgers to ensure a win for Hibs, to enhance Neil Lennon's chances of getting the Celtic job back when the first English Premier League club that shows a serious interest in him comes along and he jumps ship.
> To put the icing on the cake enhance Hibs chances of finishing second in the league and set up what Rodgers clearly believes will be an easy title party at Parkhead on Sunday when the country's biggest club and wounded giant comes calling.[4]

The only thing that was true about that deranged diatribe was that Hibs were closing in on Neo-Gers. The victory over Celtic put them level on points with Neo-Gers; only being behind them in the league table due to goal difference.[5] Neo-Gers did have a game in hand, but that game was, of course, against Celtic. Still, as one individual put it, 'Celtic think they can just turn up to beat Rangers (sic) but Graeme Murty can get Rangers (sic) up for this one and pull off a shock victory.'[6]

Not all of The People, however, shared this character's enthusiasm. 'We are gonna get pumped again,' said one.[7] But, then, the Hibs v Celtic match took place on the 21st of April; that date meant many of The People's minds were elsewhere.

Happy 92nd Birthday Ma'am.[8]

Long to reign over us…[9]

Our Sovereign Lady, God bless and protect from republican hordes, happy b'thday Maam[10]

Yes, it was Old German Liz's birthday and The People were at their sycophantic best. With another Royal brat and another Royal wedding on the way, they had plenty to tug their forelocks to. The thread on Rangers (sic) Media showed a modified picture of the Queen, bearing the legend, '6 DEED AND I'M STILL HERE'.[11] Those 'six dead' that the photoshopped plaque mentions refers to the number of popes that have died during Liz's lifetime. Everyone gets drawn into the People's bigotry.

The same thread also contains posts by folk that are 'proud' to share their birthdays with the Queen. They also share their birthdays with a famous place. Legend has it that Rome was founded by Romulus on the 21st of April 753 B.C. Do you think any of them will ever express their 'pride' at sharing their birthdays with the Eternal City?

Anyway, there wasn't as much hype over this particular game; Neo-Gers didn't have a chance in hell and everybody knew it. 5-0 was the final score and Celtic had notched up another title win.[12] There could be no excuses this time. As the Sky commentator pointed out, the Neo-Gers players didn't lack fight or courage; it was

It took another day or two for the shit to really hit the fan. Nobody placed too much blame at Murty's door; it was all the Neo-Gers' board's fault. This had been brewing for a while; even after the semi-final someone called the Daily Record Hotline to say, 'King and his cronies should hang their heads in shame. Rangers (sic) have conned their supporters season in, season out.'[28]

Honest Dave's appeal for The People to buy season-tickets had gone down like a lead balloon as well.

> King did the dirty on Murty by destroying his credibility with the team prior to the semi- final with his announcement about appointing a new manager for next season.[29]

And that wasn't the only statement from the board that caused uproar.

Not long after the 4-0 defeat at Hampden, Alastair 'Noddy' Johnston, who was a director at Neo-Gers once again, expressed the opinion that Neo-Gers were 'ahead of the curve' on the road to recovery. He said,

> In terms of looking forward from where we were four or five years ago at the bottom, the progress that has been gradually made, we are probably ahead of the curve in reality if we finish second or third.
> We are making progress. Hopefully the curve will be fast but it is still going to be gradual, it is not going to happen overnight.[30]

This was all true, but it was not what The People wanted to hear. As far as they were concerned, Neo-Gers should have been winning the Premiership in season 2016-17. The Daily Record's Neo-Gers blogger, James Black, condemned Johnston for his remarks and castigated the whole board for being 'out of touch'.[31] The People pretty much agreed with this analysis, one of them saying, 'They think we are fucking idiots.'[32]

After the match at Celtic Park, Gary Ralston, in the Daily Record, opined that Murty was a 'broken man'. He said,

Dismiss completely the notion Rangers (sic) did not put Murty up to face the media in the wake of his side's 5-0 humiliation against Celtic out of an act of petulance.

Murty was broken after this latest capitulation, so distraught there were genuine fears for his emotional wellbeing if he faced the cameras and microphones.[33]

That made it sound as if the Neo-Gers board was full of caring, sensitive souls, worried about poor Murty's feelings. Strangely, Ralston went on,

Rangers (sic) directors stuck around after watching their side trounced just long enough to congratulate Peter Lawwell and Co before heading for their cars ahead of the Celtic fans exiting from their latest Parkhead party.

How many of them took the time to consider his fragile state on Sunday afternoon and headed towards the Parkhead dressing rooms to offer emotional support as the demands of a job they should never have awarded him threaten to drown this decent man completely?

Don't be surprised if it's the same number as the aggregate amount of goals Rangers (sic) have scored against their old foes over the past fortnight in a fixture that is now only a rivalry in name.[34]

So, which one was it? Was the Neo-Gers boardroom full of philanthropic social workers or were they all heartless bastards? It looked as if Ralston couldn't make his mind up. He did recommend, though, that Murty walk out on Neo-Gers.

In fact, the Daily Record reported, on the same day, that Murty had, indeed, resigned.

Before Sunday's 5-0 defeat to Celtic the former caretaker had said he wouldn't leave before the end of the season.

But he has decided he isn't the man for the job and has decided to walk away. He is believed to have been left broken by the defeats to Celtic and was deserted by the directors after the Celtic Park mauling.[35]

This, however, was utter shite. The truth was that Murty had been sacked, or, as Neo-Gers themselves put it, 'relieved of his duties'.[36] So much for there being a caring bunch at the top of the marble stairs! The People and the agnivores continued to excoriate the Neo-Gers board and blame it for Murty's failures.

I wish the best of luck to Graeme Murty, the board that placed him in this position are as much to blame. It clearly didnt work in his favour but the board should have never have used him as a scapegoat.[37]

Graeme Murty did the best he could with what he had at Rangers (sic).
He was badly cast in the wrong movie at Ibrox by an incompetent board which hung him out to dry.
Good luck and all the best to him for the future.[38]

Murty has been treated appallingly by the Rangers (sic) board
They gave him the job, because he did well enough for them to be able to sell it to the fans without a revolt and more importantly to buy them time
Now after many incidents of being undermined he's gone....[39]

The Daily Record ran a quick survey, asking, 'Was Graeme Murty treated badly by the board?' 94% of those that took part felt that he was.[40] Meanwhile, Keith Jackson broke ranks with Level 5 to have a go at King and his board as well. Although he couldn't resist having one, last swipe at Murty, most of his ire was directed towards the Neo-Gers board.

This is a board that replaces professionals with patsies in the name of self-preservation. A regime which promised to be open and transparent but which has proven to be almost as clandestine and Machiavellian as those which clung to power before. Murty is no more than a willing accomplice to their glaring inadequacies and now he's paid the ultimate price for it.[41]

It was beginning to look as if it was time to fire up the torches, sharpen the pitchforks and get the rat masks out of mothballs. But where were the leading lights of the mob that had chased the previous board? Why weren't they up in arms along with the rest of the supporters? The blog *daviesleftpeg* set out to provide an answer.

This particular blog is as staunch as they come; full as it is of stories about 'Rangers (sic) Haters' and big conspiracies against the Ibrox club. It certainly wasn't a Jack Irvine-fed hater of all things King-related. Folk would probably pay attention, then, to what it had to say about the current Neo-Gers board and its cronies.

> Fans have been continually duped by certain individuals posing as leaders or representatives of fan organisations. Where are these individuals now? Well, almost all of them have jobs within the club. They weren't looking after us, the fans, they were serving their own best interests. Despite none of them having suitable attributes or relevant experience. Promises of riches were made for essentially pulling the wool over our eyes.[42]

The blog went on to tell of how Listy Graham, Halloween Houston and others all had their snouts in the trough. In fact, it seems that there was a lot of in-fighting among them to get the most out of their association with Neo-Gers. Not only that, but they were making deals with Honest Dave on behalf of the supporters, but without the knowledge of those supporters. And there was even more to come:

> To add to this all, despite Club 1872 being led by voluntary members, it is stated clearly in this letter Chris is being paid for his work. We call on all members of Club 1872 to seek an explanation on this and ask who is paying the wages of an unelected, racist, Islamophobe and why is he again working at our club?
> It is being suggested that payment is being met by Rangers (sic) themselves. So where exactly does that leave the independence of the organisation? Answers must be given.[43]

Finally, some of The People were realising that they had been, and were being, conned. There was no fan representation on the board and it looked as if the board was manipulating the main supporters' group for its own end. Indeed, it looked as if conning the supporters was the whole *raison d'être* of Club 1872 right from the very start. No wonder the rat masks were conspicuous by their absence this time round!

Another member of the Neo-Gers support was scathing about the board as well, with his fellow forum members on *FollowFollow* agreeing with him.

> There is an ever increasing chasm between our board and the support metastasising into anger and a lack of trust. These are estranged emotions to harbour towards the men who have done so much, but frankly, they have dined out on the accolades for long enough. We were promised vision, strategy, transparency, but most importantly: action. We see none of these things at a time while the most average of Celtic teams canter and swagger towards the easiest back to back trebles, while we are managed by a nervous and unconvincing u-20 coach, our captain and vice-captain are suspended, but we are still targeting players who don't know who they will be playing for?[44]

The rather ironic thing is that, while elements of The People banged on about the lack of leadership and vision inside Ibrox, the same problem existed on the outside as well. The People, by their very nature, are follow-followers, ready to throw their support behind any snake-oil salesman that says the right things. A few folk had, uncharacteristically, stepped up to the plate to get rid of the 'rats' and usher in the King regime. Unfortunately, it now seems that they were followers as well, working under the orders of Honest Dave.

There was some talk of not renewing season tickets but they all needed somebody to *tell* them what they should do. They were angry but had nobody to follow; who could they trust? It was the ideal opportunity for any major shareholders that wanted rid of King to step into the breach and appoint their own versions of Listy Graham and Halloween Houston.

Honest Dave, however, didn't get where he is today without being able to play people at the appropriate time. Things seemed to be going against him, but he was more than equal to the task. He needed to get The People back onside and it proved to be a remarkably easy thing to do.

10
Ever Fallen in Love (With Someone You Shouldn't've?)

I f you've seen *Life of Brian*, then you'll know how folk could be duped into believing anyone is the Messiah. Unlike the reluctant Brian, there were plenty in the ancient world that claimed to be the long-awaited Saviour. People might follow them, or they might not; most were laughed at and many ended up suffering the same fate as Brian and Jesus. But this belief in a great deliverer wasn't just confined to the Jews.

Ancient people didn't live in a vacuum and, just as in modern times, many were interested in finding out about other cultures. This curiosity might have been the preserve of the rich, who were able to travel, but bits and pieces filtered down to ordinary folk as well. The messianic stories of the Jews took seed and grew into a belief that a Great King was going to rise in the East to drive off the yoke of Roman imperialism.

Mithridates VI of Pontus was able to make use of such tales to rally different peoples of the Middle East to his side in his wars against Rome. In the main, though, every petty chieftain with a grudge and pirate captain with pretensions of grandeur, claimed to be the promised one and, consequently, called themselves 'King'.

People in the ancient world, however, weren't all as simple-minded and superstitious as you might think and practically all of these 'messiahs' had no great following and have been totally forgotten and ignored by history. There are people in our modern age, by contrast, that are as gullible as they come and are willing to follow just about anybody.

Imagine living like one of these folk, following some guru that's told you the world's going to end in a week's time. It's hard to think that you'd actually be disappointed to see the sun coming up and realise that you and your family aren't going to die after all. Then, you'd have to rush home, if you've still got one, get ready and go in and beg for your job back. But, when the Great Leader admits he was wrong and gives you a revised date for Armageddon, you'll do the whole thing all over again.

It seems that some folk, no matter how many disappointments they get in life, will be ready to make the same mistakes all over again. Such a crew is The People. How many 'saviours' have they strewn palm fronds in front of? How many chairmen and managers have turned up at Ibrox in triumph, only to leave under a cloud? And yet, The People turn up every time to wave their Union flags and sing their vile songs of triumphalism. You can't even feel sorry for them. As the old saying goes, stupidity is doing the same thing over and over and expecting a different result.

Life for The People revolves around two things: a humongously rich benefactor pouring money into their club and beating Celtic. They look back to the glory days when their old club was winning everything but refuse to accept that David Murray wasn't bankrolling it all. And since they believe that the new club is still the old one, they're desperately awaiting 'another' benefactor; even though they've actually never had one. Failing some gazillionaire coming on the scene, they'll settle for beating Celtic.

In fact, if they do manage to beat Celtic in the Premiership, they imagine that all the riches of the Champions League are theirs for the taking. After that, everything else would fall into place; sponsorship deals, increased sales of replica kits etc. In this respect, all they need is a decent manager.

The rumours about Steven Gerrard coming to Neo-Gers started even before the 5-0 game at Celtic Park. It seems the bookies slashed the odds of Gerrard becoming Neo-Gers boss from 25/1 into 8/1.[1] This suggested that somebody knew something the rest of us didn't and was cashing in on that knowledge. Those odds were slashed even further when Honest Dave turned up at Anfield for the Champions League semi-final. Of course, King has never made any secret of his liking for Liverpool FC, so his presence there could have been perfectly innocent.[2] Or he might have just been desperate to hear *Zadok the Priest*. After all, he was hardly likely to hear it at Ibrox anytime soon.

The speculation, however, was intensified by the fact that Gerrard had appeared at Ibrox to watch Neo-Gers being beaten by Celtic. Most folk shrugged and passed off Gerrard being at Ibrox and King at Anfield as coincidence; Gerrard couldn't be stupid enough to take the Neo-Gers job, could he? And why would Neo-Gers replace a failing Under-20s coach with a rookie Under-18s one? If Murty thought anything of the rumours, he must have been blazing.

Chris Sutton predicted that the whole thing would end in tears, calling the Neo-Gers job, 'The most poisoned chalice around.' He also remarked of Gerrard,

> He's got less experience than Graeme Murty, who is being hunted out of the club and told he's not good enough because he, er, doesn't have enough experience.[3]

Some of The People expressed doubts as well.

> Appointing someone with no managerial experience on a shoe-string budget just isn't the answer as far as I'm concerned. He may be a big name but he's not the answer.[4]

> It is beyond belief Rangers are considering a manager with no experience and no knowledge of the Scottish game.[5]

> If Rangers appoint a rookie coach such as Gerrard then we've all but given Celtic 10-in-a-row. It's nothing against Gerrard as he could be a brilliant manager in the future, but we need an experienced man in.[6]

Despite this negativity, talks appeared to be progressing between Gerrard and Neo-Gers, with the Liverpool Under-18s boss supposedly keen to take up the post. All bets were finally off on the 4th May when Gerrard arrived at Ibrox to put pen to paper. He said,

104

I am honoured to become the next manager of Rangers (sic). I have enormous respect for this football club, and its history and tradition.

I can't wait to start this new journey at Rangers (sic) as we look to build on the many successes that this club has achieved.[7]

It looked as if Gerrard had already subscribed to the Big Lie. It was no doubt a condition of accepting the job; it would also probably be his downfall. Already he was talking about the 'many successes' of a club that had only ever won a Petrofac Cup. He should, perhaps, have paid attention to what John Barnes said,

...it's not because Steven is inexperienced, it's not because he's not managed anyone. If he doesn't challenge Celtic straight away it's got nothing to do with his ability.[8]

The agnivores and The People just concentrated on the parts where Barnes said that even the best managers couldn't turn Neo-Gers around overnight. To them, he was just another nay-sayer, predicting that Gerrard was going to be a spectacular failure. In fact, he was only stressing what others were already saying; Gerrard would need to be given time, not just resources. The ex-Liverpool player signed a four-year contract; he was expected, however, to succeed immediately.

The People turned up to Ibrox to welcome yet another 'messiah'. You'd have thought they'd be sick of it by now; but, no. They waved their scarves and flags, as they had done many times before,[9] while outside, they serenaded their new hero with a chorus of *The Billy Boys*.[10] As well as waving to the crowds, Gerrard was shown round Ibrox, where a rather embarrassing episode occurred.

Jimmy Bell has been the kitman at Ibrox probably since the *Gallant Pioneers* first set up Rangers. He 'TUPEd' over to Charles Green's new club and still sets out the strips every second weekend. He is, unfortunately, a renowned bigot, who refused to deal with Mo Johnston's strip when he played for Rangers. Bell's meeting with Gerrard was recorded by Neo-Gers TV for everyone to see. It was an extremely awkward few minutes.[11]

Bell's reaction was no doubt due to the fact that Gerrard attended an RC school, has a daughter called 'Lourdes' and has been a well-known

105

fan of Celtic for years. Somebody, however, did a bit of digging and discovered that, although he attended an RC school, Gerrard was not, in fact, a Catholic.[12] This information was presented as a joke, but it would certainly put Bell and his fellow bigots' minds at rest. As my mother used to say, 'Half in fun, whole in earnest.'

Honest Dave had managed to play The People yet again. Those moans and groans about the Neo-Gers board gradually turned to more positive noises.

> I'm reliably informed serious investors are looking to put money into Rangers and give Gerrard a decent transfer kitty. Watch this space.[13]

We didn't need to watch that space; Honest Dave said, on the day Gerrard was introduced to the hordes, that he was going to reveal all three days later on the Monday. We'd eventually find out if all the online boasting about Chinese and American investors by The People was true or not. Keith Jackson made it plain that King was going to have to come up with something special.

> On Friday he talked fleetingly of raising cash through a share issue but for as long as his dispute with the Takeover Panel remains ongoing, this seems no more than wishful thinking.[14]

Unbelievably, raising cash through a share issue was all that King had to offer. At best, this was going to give Gerrard £6m to work with; hardly a sum that was going to be enough to overtake Celtic. The People's gas was soon put at a peep when King revealed that they were kidding themselves about foreign investors.

> At this stage there is nothing external other than existing shareholders and existing investors. We're not talking to anyone new who's not there already.[15]

And that was that. Except it wasn't. Surely Steven Gerrard hadn't fallen for a load of flimflam from King? Nobody could be that stupid, surely. Footballers, generally, aren't renowned for being over-endowed with grey matter and Gerrard, it seems, is no exception. *The*

Green Jhedi, a regular commenter on my blog, posted a link to a recording of some radio programme, where Gerrard, when asked his favourite cheese, replied, 'Melted.'[16] And then there was his coaching course, of which he stated,

> A lot of ex-players over the years have been put off by the amount of work you have to put in on the [coaching] courses.
> I think [in the past] it was almost a test on the courses and people were intimidated to fail and didn't want to be put in the spotlight in front of all the other people that were on the course.[17]

In other words, the courses had been made a lot easier and even somebody with a dearth of brain cells, like Gerrard, could cope. It didn't say much for the courses or the folk that had been through them. Perhaps Gerrard wasn't the shrewd operator everybody seemed to think.

It was hard to see how Gerrard was going to get any cash at all. Keith Jackson was right about the share issue, no matter what King himself might say. On 3rd of May, it was reported that the Takeover Panel had obtained a court order to force King to make his mandatory offer in the proper fashion. There was to be no more messing about; funds had to be placed in an escrow account, with a third, independent, party verifying that they were available.[18]

Almost immediately, Neo-Gers Directors Barry Scott and, incredibly, Paul Murray, resigned from the board.[19] It would be a remarkable coincidence if the two things weren't connected. Paul Murray, Scotland's answer to Beau Brummell, had been involved in Rangers for years and took part in more than one attempt to take over Rangers while it was in administration, and then Neo-Gers, when the old club died. It would have to be something serious to make him pack up his hairspray and leave.

King spoke of how the Takeover Panel and the mandatory offer would have no effect on any share issue.

> Just to finally cover the Takeover Panel, it is important to stress this has absolutely nothing whatsoever in any way to do with the football club, directly or indirectly.

It makes no difference to the football club, it makes no difference to the funding of the football club, it makes no difference to the ownership of the football club. This is an issue between myself and the shareholders of the holding company. It has got nothing to do with Rangers (sic), it has got nothing to do with the team, nothing to do with funding.[20]

The phrase, he 'doth protest too much, methinks', springs to mind. In fact, as King himself admitted, he would not be allowed to play any part in the share issue.[21] This, of course, begs the question as to who was going to underwrite the issue. This is a serious point since every share issue to The People has always been undersubscribed. And as for institutional investors, why would they buy shares in a company that's not listed on any market? There's no way of knowing if your share price is going up or down; indeed, there was only King's word for it that the shares were worth more than 20p.

I don't profess to know how all this financial business works, but it seems to me that if there was to be an issue at 27p per share and, thereafter, those shares would be worth only half the equity they were beforehand, then that means the shares must be worth 54p before the issue. I'm probably wrong, but there's no way of knowing for certain; the shares don't appear on any market listing.

Any prospectus wouldn't be able to outline how the shares have performed and certainly couldn't make predictions. Purchasers would be buying a pig in a poke, not knowing if they've been swindled or not. It hardly looked like an attractive investment. More than likely, current shareholders would be following over themselves to hand over their shares for 20p each when King made his mandatory offer.

But, even if we allowed that King knew what he was doing, and he *did* raise £6m from a share issue, it was still not enough for Gerrard to make any kind of dent in Celtic's dominance. Barry Ferguson pointed this out but felt that 'There will be something in the pipeline they are working on'.[22] There's that blind hope The People are famous for. It was hard to see where any other funding could possibly come from. Of course, they could always sell some of the squad.

108

This is what Ian Durrant suggested was going to happen. He predicted a mass clear-out, as happened when Graeme Souness arrived at Ibrox.[23] According to Durrant, fifteen players left the club within a week of Souness arriving.[24] Maybe old age is beginning to affect his memory, but Durrant was talking shite. The 'Souness Revolution' didn't happen overnight.

In the 1985-86 season, there were twenty-two players in the Rangers squad.[25] Only six of those moved on in 1986 and another six went to pastures new in 1987. Even the 'Souness Revolution' took time to get fully into its stride. Yes, Rangers won the title in 1987, but it wasn't until 1988-89 that they started their dominance of Scottish football.

Even if he did attempt to have a mass clear-out, Gerrard would be stymied by the fact that nobody was going to want the players he had. Even if anybody did fancy any of them, they certainly wouldn't be paying the kind of prices that would give Gerrard a decent warchest. King had probably told Gerrard that he'd get millions for Morales; and Gerrard was daft enough to believe him. Meanwhile, there were high earners at Neo-Gers that would be going nowhere.

Carlos Peña, for example was under contract until 2020 and there would be no getting rid of him. His loan spell at Cruz Azul was nothing short of a disaster[26] and absolutely nobody would be stupid enough to sign him permanently. Then there was Bruno Alves, who, despite his reputation, hadn't made much of an impact. His contract ran until 2019 and neither he nor anybody else had made any noises about him moving.

Mexican club Chivas had promised to take Eduardo Herrera off Neo-Gers' hands in the summer window, but they certainly wouldn't be paying over the odds. As the Daily Record put it, 'Now the Guadalajara club are set to make a move to allow Rangers (sic) to cut their losses on the striker.'[27] That phrase pretty much confirmed that Gerrard wouldn't be getting any funds from that particular sale.

The agnivores saw no reason to hang about waiting for somebody to buy the Neo-Gers Action Man's Heids. 'Eduardo Herrara, Fabio Cardoso, Andy Halliday, Jak Alnwick, Joe Dodoo, Bruno Alves and Michael O'Halloran are expected to be shown the door.'[28] Things weren't quite that simple, though. It wouldn't just be a matter of sacking this lot; the remainder of their contracts would have to be paid. That would probably take care of most of the cash raised in the shares issue.

It was made out as if Dalcio was just the start of a flood and that the rest would be following him in the summer. It seemed as if Dalcio was happy to go for free, implying that the others would be similarly altruistic.[29] In the article it was quickly mentioned in a 'blink and you'll miss it' kind of way that Dalcio had been on loan from Benfica. His loan period was over; that was the only reason he was leaving. He certainly wasn't the start of a mass exodus; the others would want their money before they went anywhere.

Of course, there was always the multi-millions that Morelos would bring in, wasn't there? We'd soon discover whether all those ridiculous stories about Chinese clubs were true or not. The probability was that they weren't, and Neo-Gers would be lucky to get a couple of million for a player who wasn't able to perform when it mattered. There might, however, be a few bob available from the sale of other players.

Already, the rumours were starting, with the agnivores claiming that both Cardiff and Burnley were looking to sign Josh Windass for around £3m.[30] We'd heard this kind of thing so many times before, however, that it was difficult to believe that it was true. Even if it were, £3m was hardly going to pay for a challenge to Celtic.

There was a clue to a likely scenario at Neo-Gers when a kite was flown in the middle of May, testing which way the wind might be blowing. Jimmy Nicholl, who was left in charge at Neo-Gers when Murty was sacked, gave 'his opinion' on the coming changes under Gerrard.

> Hopefully, not a massive change. What I mean by that is that he will get something out of the existing squad.
> Yes, some of them will be gone but if he gets something out of the existing ones, he won't need too many new players.
> I hope he doesn't need eight or nine. I hope in the end he only needs three or four.
> He should get more out of the boys who are here. If they have anything about them, then he will do. They will respond to his demands.[31]

At this point, Nicholl had probably already made his mind up to leave Neo-Gers,[32] so he had nothing to gain or lose by his statement to the Evening Times. It looked as if he was spouting somebody's else's ideas, to see how The People would react. The fact that there was no outrage forthcoming suggested that it might well be something that the Neo-Gers supporters would go along with. That meant no, or very few, new signings and certainly no mass clear-out.

This didn't stop the agnivores making speculations about the folk that Gerrard was going to sign. These included Martin Skrtel of Fenerbahce[33] and John McGinn of Hibs.[34] These signings seemed highly unlikely since Hibs wanted at least £5m for McGinn[35] and Fenerbahce had no intention of selling Skrtel.[36] The most ridiculous story involved Wayne Rooney going to Ibrox; something that was never going to happen.[37]

More likely was the story that Gerrard intended making a loan move for young, Liverpool striker Dominic Solanke.[38] In fact, if Neo-Gers were serious about stopping Celtic, then loan deals were probably the only way they could possibly do it. Even that, though, would cost more money than they had; unless they could persuade the parent clubs to keep paying their players.

Whatever was going to happen, The People were all excited again. There was no more talk of not renewing season tickets or handing Celtic ten-in-a-row. Instead, things had changed to:

> It's a great bit of business to get Gerrard. It's a pick-me-up as a fan and I know a few Celtic fans aren't happy as that's 10-in-a-row off the menu.[39]

Now, that *was* a turnaround. All The People were over the moon about Gerrard and, yet again, all was forgiven as far as Honest Dave was concerned. Even *daviesleftpeg* seemed to agree that King deserved one, last chance.[40] We'd all seen this movie before. Things were being set up, again, for The People to suffer yet more hurt and disappointment. As usual, though, they only had themselves to blame.

11
Love Is Lies

Back in August, the Daily Record had an article that everyone would have had a quiet snigger at. It seemed that all the roads around Ibrox Stadium would be closed during Neo-Gers home matches. This was because the 'UK Threat Level for international terrorism is severe which means an attack is highly likely.'[1] These restrictions would be staying in place until it was deemed that a terrorist attack was less likely. Doubtless anti-terrorist police would be on patrol as well.

Strangely, the same terrorist threat didn't seem to affect any other footballing venue, including Hampden. Only The People and the agnivores would believe that their club would be a viable target for ISIS and the like. No doubt their belief in being the 'Quintessentially British club' would, in their minds, mean that it would be the Number 1 target of Islamic fundamentalists.

In truth, it was just another desperate attempt by Neo-Gers, and their pals in the media, to make the new club appear relevant. It was quite risible to suggest that terrorists worldwide had even heard of the Ibrox club, let alone make plans to attack it.

Only a few months later, in March, the agnivores were singing a different tune. Apparently, it was unfair that Neo-Gers had to pay more for policing than any other club or even the SFA.[2] Surely if those anti-terror squads were sent back to the ports and airports, where they belonged, instead of wasting their time walking around Govan, then Neo-Gers wouldn't be paying quite so much! As usual, it was their own hubris that was causing the problems. And, as usual, the agnivores wouldn't report that this was the case.

In the few years since Neo-Gers' creation, the Scottish sports media had settled down to a cosy relationship, reminiscent of the days of succulent lamb. Jabba, like a huge, fat spider, would sit, spinning his Level5 lies and the agnivores would repeat them, practically verbatim, in their newspapers and TV and radio programmes.

The story of Alfredo Morelos attracting huge bids from Chinese football clubs was just one instance where the agnivores fell into line. As we saw in Chapter 4, one brave fellow stuck his head over the parapet to say that nobody in China was bidding for Morelos.[3] He was soon slapped down and fell back into the ranks almost immediately.

The story paraded in all the papers was that Morelos wasn't for sale at any price; he was staying at Neo-Gers. The purpose of this spin from Jabba's web was twofold: it showed that Neo-Gers didn't need the money and it proved how ambitious the club was when it was holding onto its 'prize asset'.[4] It was a load of fertiliser and they knew it; but they'd go to any lengths to keep The People happy.

In stark contrast, there were constant stories about Celtic players being on the way out. The claim by SKY that Moussa Dembélé had been sold to Brighton was just one of the desperate fictions, calculated to unsettle Celtic and its players.[5] Even Brendan Rodgers wasn't immune to the agnivores trying to sell him on. All he did was explain why he might be considered for the Arsenal job and it was blown up as him throwing his hat into the ring.[6]

This ridiculous agenda by the agnivores was made all the more ludicrous when one looked at the facts. Celtic had no need to sell anyone and nobody, least of all the manager, had expressed any desire to leave. In contrast, Neo-Gers were skint and would have bitten the hand off anyone offering silly money for Morelos. The story the press was selling, though, was that Neo-Gers was a settled, ambitious club while at Celtic, everybody couldn't wait to get out and the whole team was in jeopardy from predatory English clubs. It was so transparent, but The People lapped it up like mother's milk.

Where the agnivores excelled, though, was in doing the dirty jobs that Neo-Gers couldn't do themselves. Remember how desperate Neo-Gers were to sign Derek McInnes as manager? The Aberdeen chairman, Stewart Milne, was having none of it, leaving Neo-Gers in a quandary. 'Tapping up', speaking to a manager or player behind his club's back, is frowned upon in football and some quite hefty fines can be handed out if you're caught doing it. There was no way Neo-Gers was going to be able to afford that; so, what were they to do? Step forward the agnivores.

Neo-Gers didn't need to do any 'tapping-up' when the media were there to do it for them. Poor Boxy's arse was barely out the door before we were hearing that Derek McInnes was the main candidate.[7]

Others went further, with even Chris Sutton saying, 'It would be absolutely the right move, Derek McInnes is the man for the job.'[8]

All through November, the papers were full of articles beseeching McInnes to take the Neo-Gers post. They told him how he would make a huge difference at Ibrox and how much they needed him. Some of them pointed out that it was his duty, nay, destiny, as a 'Real Rangers Man' to help Neo-Gers in its hour of need. This nonsense culminated in Keith Jackson's assertion that McInnes was ready to quit Aberdeen for the Neo-Gers job.[9]

So sure of the job they had done were the agnivores that they were certain that McInnes couldn't possibly give Neo-Gers a knock-back. Jackson quoted a 'source' that said,

> He (McInnes) now faces a difficult decision but if he wants to be the next manager of Rangers (sic) – and it seems very much that he does – then he knows now what he has to do.
> It looks as if things could become legally messy between Derek and Aberdeen. He may have to take a leap of faith where Gers are concerned. But this opportunity looks impossible to turn down.[10]

As we know, McInnes stayed at Aberdeen, but the agnivores had tried their best. In fact, they probably went too far. As Jackson's 'source' put it,

> Rangers (sic) haven't exactly helped to make it a smooth passage down the road and Stewart Milne clearly feels, because of the way they have gone about their business, he has no choice but to take a stand.[11]

But, really, Neo-Gers had done nothing. It had been all the agnivores' own work, no doubt orchestrated by Jabba. Unlike The People, the agnivores took the lesson to heart and were less intensive, to the point of hardly mentioning it, when it came to the next Neo-Gers target.

Steve Clarke, the manager at Kilmarnock, seemed an obvious fit; he had dragged a failing team up from the very bottom of the league and had made it one of the few teams to beat Celtic.[12] That, in itself, was enough to convince The People. It wasn't long before they were clamouring for Neo-Gers to get Clarke on board for next season.[13] The agnivores, though, backed off a bit, merely reporting that The People wanted Clarke.[14]

It seems that Neo-Gers *did* sound out Steve Clarke about moving to Ibrox but were turned down flat.[15] Clarke was, no doubt, aware of Derek McInnes turning the job down and, since folk talk to each other, he probably knew what it was that put the Aberdeen manager off. Of course, all this was forgotten in the rush to praise the signing of Steven Gerrard.

As well as the signing of Gerrard, which was presented as a great coup, the agnivores were also over the moon about Neo-Gers' new kit deal. While they were all gushing about the deal with *Hummel*, the Daily Record published an article that cast doubt on the new supplier being one of the 'big boys'. It also cast doubt on Neo-Gers being a big club. Expert Neal Heard said, 'No disrespect to Rangers (sic) but the likes of Nike are too big for them now.'[16]

Heard went on, in an apologetic and diplomatic vein, to point out that *Hummel* was taking a huge gamble on Neo-Gers. The hope was that the club would do a lot better in the future and *Hummel* would be quids in. Apparently, *Nike* and the rest of the bigger manufacturers have clauses in their contracts that allow them to cancel if the team gets relegated. 'A lot of it is to do with how it effects on their brand, not all of them want to have clubs that aren't doing well.'[17] In other words, *Nike* doesn't associate with losers.

The People were suitably unimpressed with Neal Heard's words. 'See this cunt in the d***y r****d saying we're not big enough for Nike.......cunt looks like he's running a stall at the barras ffs'.[18] Jabba, no doubt, felt pretty much the same and let his feelings be known. You'll have noticed that my link to the Daily Record story doesn't actually go to the Daily Record. That's because they've deleted the article.[19] Did a certain, fat denizen of Blythswood Square tell them to?

One of the recurring themes in the Scottish media ever since Rangers died, indeed, even when they went into administration, has been that Scottish football needs a 'strong Rangers (sic)'. Strangely, when Celtic were at death's door and Rangers were dominant in the 1990s nobody claimed that a strong Celtic was needed. It's not clear how they expect Neo-Gers to suddenly get stronger, unless they're thinking of them receiving money from the state or a special tax is imposed on Celtic.

All manner of ex-players and managers have been wheeled out to support this widely-accepted nonsense, including a few soup-taking ex-Celtic players. It was a surprise to find among the latter the legend that is Stiliyan Petrov. His take on things was that,

> Celtic have a lot of young, exciting players. These players would like to improve and be challenged.
>
> If they are not challenged here, if they don't have someone to push them, then they will go. Can you blame them? No.
>
> If someone comes in for Dembele and he is not being challenged here then he will move on.[20]

This is pish of the lowest calibre and it makes you wonder if Stan has fallen on hard times if he's accepting payment for this kind of thing.

Still, this maxim had its critics, even among the agnivores; or, at least, it appeared so. 'Rangers (sic) have no God-given right to be the one that challenges Celtic',[21] said the sub-headline to a Gordon Waddell article that had nothing to do with that topic. In fact, Waddell was expressing his, and possibly The People's, fears that Gerrard was going to be yet another failure, although he evidently hoped not. Even apart from that headline, it looked as if Waddell was distancing himself from the Jabba-fed good news.

The reason for this is rather obvious. While The People are content to swallow the Gospel according to Jabba, the rest of us aren't quite so gullible. Even some of The People have managed to evolve from the happy state of their fellow supporters into creatures with a handful of brain cells, who question whether all the sycophancy is masking the truth. The odd article that goes against the grain helps to maintain the illusion that Scotland's sports writers are working independently and untrammelled.

The fact that the headline doesn't match what's in the article is quite a different matter. The Daily Record is aware of its readership and knows that most of it has neither the ability nor the patience to work its way through a whole article. Such folk will take half an hour to read the headline and sub-headline and leave it at that. The

Record has made an art-form out of providing sound-bites for these imbeciles.

For example, Brendan Rodgers opened up to the Evening Times in May, saying, 'I had this fear of complacency. It's a fear I always have.'[22] Rodgers had said this kind of thing before, when he was manager of Liverpool.[23] He also told the Daily Record the same thing in April, on the day of the Scottish Cup semi-final. The Record headed the piece with the legend: 'Celtic boss Brendan Rodgers reveals fear of failure against Rangers (sic) is what drives him on'.[24] In the article it's clear that Rodgers said no such thing. That headline, though, would cheer up all the Neo-Gers knuckle-draggers, who would now believe that Rodgers was running scared of their club.

And then there was Steven Gerrard. The Liverpudlian's arrival at Ibrox was trumpeted as the biggest thing to happen in Scottish football in its entire history. Forget the time Celtic became the first team in the whole of northern Europe to win the European Cup; this was much bigger than that. You couldn't open a paper without seeing Gerrard's name popping out on every page. It seemed that not only was he coming to save Neo-Gers, but the whole of Scottish football. And that was only the start. He was going to sort out all the problems in the Middle East, end world hunger and bring peace to the whole of humanity.

James Black, the Daily Record's 'Rangers (sic) blogger', had this to say,

> Steven Gerrard's appointment as Rangers (sic) manager had the entire world talking about Scottish football for the first time in years.
> It quickly reminded everyone that, for all of their success under Brendan Rodgers, Celtic are very much still playing second-fiddle in Glasgow.[25]

This, of course, is a load of delusional crap. Maybe Black doesn't realise, but the whole purpose of a football team is to win; not to get tongues wagging. He went on,

> The Liverpool icon's imminent arrival has generated headlines from Los Angeles to Tokyo, and pretty much

117

everywhere in between, and is a genuine box-office signing that is going to make next season much more interesting for both sides.

Everybody has been talking about the Rangers (sic) manager - with some of the biggest names in football tweeting their congratulations - while Celtic securing seven in a row barely merited a mention outside of Scotland.[26]

I don't think they get the Daily Record and Evening Times in Los Angeles and Tokyo and I seriously doubt if most Americans and Japanese even know who Steven Gerrard is, let alone the team he's going to manage. Black would do well to remember the last time Neo-Gers was the big talking-point down in England. It was when they signed a certain Joey Barton; and we all know how that ended.

Gordon Parks, in the Daily Record, meanwhile, took a different tack. In one of those 'look-at-me-I'm-independently-minded' pieces, he argued that Gerrard should be nowhere near Neo-Gers. He had no real experience as a manager and should be like other young managers, 'cutting their teeth at small clubs, doing a Michael O'Neill at Brechin and following the path taken by Jack Ross at Alloa.'[27] He certainly shouldn't be starting out at a 'big club' like Neo-Gers.

But, wait…this was the same character that had told us that Patrick Roberts showed a 'lack of ambition' by coming back to Celtic. He said,

…why turn down the chance to play a season in La Liga with Girona or head to France with Nice instead of plying his trade at Firhill, Dingwall and the plastic of Hamilton and Kilmarnock?[28]

In other words, Roberts chose to play at a wee team like Celtic, against inferior opposition, instead of 'operating in a different footballing stratosphere' like other young players. He ended by saying, 'Paradise is no place to reach for the stars.'[29]

So, let's see if we've got this right. Celtic is a wee team, playing in a backwater, and should be given a bodyswerve by anyone that's serious about their footballing career. Meanwhile, Neo-Gers is too big a club for a world-class player like Gerrard to be starting out on the road to management. Er…has Parks looked at the placings in the Scottish Premiership table?

On the 15th of May, Gerrard made his first signing, before he'd even started officially as Neo-Gers manager. Scott Arfield arrived, to much fanfare, with the message that, 'Gerrard will definitely attract top players.'[30] What kind of 'top player' did he mean? Himself? Arfield was a free transfer, leaving Burnley at the end of a contract that they didn't bother to renew. He might have been considered something of a big deal at one time, but, in the 2017-18 season, Arfield only played for 1335 minutes.[31] That might sound like a lot but try dividing it by 90!

Despite the accolades coming from the agnivores, it looked like the usual Action Man's Heids would be turning up at Auchenhowie for training. It certainly looked as if Brendan Rodgers had nothing to lose any sleep over.

The vile bias of the agnivores was laid bare in all its putrescence after the last day of the league season. Shay Logan, of Aberdeen, is reminiscent of El-Hadji Diouf in the way he desperately wants to be seen as the 'bad boy' of Scottish football, especially in front of the Celtic Support. James Forrest sums him up pretty accurately.[32] He ended up with a red card at the end of the Celtic v Aberdeen final-day clash. He tried to taunt the Celtic supporters and then started lashing out at players. Here's what the Scotsman had to say about his behaviour:

> There has been a mutual dislike between Logan and the Parkhead faithful since the Englishman was victim of racial abuse by Celtic's Aleksandar Tonev during a league game in 2014.[33]

Actually, he was an *alleged* victim of racial abuse, but the football authorities, with no corroborating evidence, decided to believe him over Tonev. There's far more to the dislike of him by Celtic supporters than that, as James Forrest's blog makes clear. But let's not dwell on that; rather, let's consider the implication made by that Scotsman article. It almost seems as if they're excusing his behaviour; it's as if he was quite right to mock and goad a crowd of supporters that hates his guts.

While this match at Parkhead was going on, another game was taking place at Easter Road. Hibs were playing Neo-Gers, in a match that would help decide who would finish in second place. It was looking at one point as if Neo-Gers were going to win, but Hibs managed to score an equaliser. Neil Lennon then ran onto a deserted part of the pitch to celebrate, running around with his arms out, like an aeroplane. He was sent to the stands for this little display. Lennon was philosophical about being sent off, saying,

> Well they make it personal, don't they?' he said afterwards. 'You all hear it. They are singing sectarian songs at me. It's just a little bit of 'have some of that'. It was worth it! Trust me.[34]

The agnivores, however, didn't see things as cut-and-dried as that. Look at the words they use.

> Neil Lennon insists he should escape punishment for his on-pitch celebration after *accusing* the Rangers support of targeting him with sectarian abuse.[35] (My italics.)

> Sectarianism was thrust to the top of the agenda once again amidst both Neil Lennon's *claims* he was the victim of sectarian taunts and Hibs fans unfurling of an offensive banner during Sunday's powderkeg clash with Rangers at Easter Road.[36] (My italics.)

It was almost as if they didn't believe what Lennon was saying. No mitigation for him, it appeared, even though the hatred of The People for him was long-standing and had even resulted in makeshift bombs being sent through the post. The words 'claims' and 'accusing' also suggested that only Lennon could hear what The People were saying, as if sibilant whispers were emanating from the crowd near the dugout. In truth, only the completely deaf could fail to hear the bile that was being directed at the Hibs manager.

So, it was okay for Logan to rile up the Celtic support, and potentially cause serious trouble, because, well, you know him and the Celtic supporters! Meanwhile, Neil Lennon answered all the bigotry being thrown at him by simply celebrating a goal. And yet, he was the only one that was in the wrong. As was said in one of Neo-Gers' many statements – it beggars belief.

It's also notable that no mention could be made about the 'claims' of the sectarian singing and chanting by The People without pointing the finger at Hibs as well. As you'll no doubt know, or have guessed, said banner had the word 'Hun' on it. Although this has been proven to be non-sectarian in a court of law, that doesn't stop The People and the agnivores presenting it as an equivalent of the filthy bigotry pouring from the stands at Ibrox. But, then, we've been over this ground a million times before.

Finally, a rather strange thing happened on the 13th of May. It was like the fall of the Berlin Wall, and the end of Apartheid in South Africa rolled into one, so world-shattering was it. Keith Jackson posted the following on Twitter:

> Jim Traynor. The simgle biggest problem Steven Gerrard
> will have to deal with at Rangers (sic).
> *single*[37]

My God! We know the agnivores like to pretend that they work independently, but that was taking things too far! Was Jet Jackson turning on his old boss, mentor and line-feeder? Probably not. That spelling mistake, 'simgle', was a clue to what most folk believed had happened. It reminded me of the *Television Personalities'* song *Where's Bill Grundy Now?*,[38] which was about the TV presenter's infamous interview with the *Sex Pistols*. Two lines in particular stand out:

> *They said he'd had too much to drink.*
> *They said that he just could not think straight.*

No doubt, Jackson woke up with a hangover and then the memory suddenly hit him of what he'd done. Like nearly everybody else, he'd have had to make an abject, grovelling apology.

12
What Do I Get?

With Celtic having the title wrapped up, all that was left was to see which teams would be taking part in the qualifying rounds for the Europa League. On that fateful Sunday when Neo-Gers were slaughtered at Celtic Park, Aberdeen were in second place with 68 points. Neo-Gers and Hibs were equal on 65 points, but the Ibrox club had the better goal difference.[1] With three games left, it was all to play for.

Back in the days when it used to be the European Cup Winners' Cup, if the winners of the Scottish Cup had also won the league, then the runners-up in the final would qualify. All that had changed and now the situation was that the losers of the Scottish Cup final qualified for nothing. Instead, that place went to the team that was fourth-place in the league.

This was a potential nightmare scenario for The People. If their team was to finish fourth in the league, then they would be faced with the unpalatable situation of needing Celtic to win the Scottish Cup to qualify for Europe. Such an outcome barely deserved thinking about.

Neo-Gers laid down a marker on the 5th of May with a lucky 1-0 defeat of Kilmarnock at home,[2] while Aberdeen and Hibs played out a goalless draw at Pittodrie.[3] It didn't make a difference to the table placings, but now Neo-Gers were only one point behind Aberdeen, with Hibs two points behind Neo-Gers. There were only two games left and all three teams were still bullish about their chances of finishing second.

Aberdeen were at home again on the Tuesday, this time against their main rivals for second place, Neo-Gers. The match ended 1-1, with Aberdeen scoring from the penalty spot, meaning that there was still only one point between the two teams.[4] Hibs were playing at Tynecastle the following evening and a victory there would mean they were back on level terms with Neo-Gers and it would all go down to the wire. Neil Lennon's team could even go second, if

Aberdeen were to slip up in their final game, which happened to be away at Celtic Park.

Hearts, during the 2017-18 season, had developed a reputation for being a gang of thugs. What the sports hacks like to call 'crunching tackles' and 'meaty challenges', which are euphemisms for out-and-out assaults, were *de rigeur* at Tynecastle. It was business as usual when Celtic came calling. A blatant assault on Scott Brown by Steven Naismith went unpunished,[5] while Craig Levein indulged in a bit of gamesmanship by putting the lawnmower out to…er…grass and leaving the pitch looking like an African savannah.[6]

Hearts did cut the grass before the Hibs game,[7] but they were just as dirty as they normally were. Hibs ended up losing 2-1 to this band of gorillas. Kyle Lafferty, who scored the first goal, should have been sent off early in the game, which must have annoyed Hibs immensely.[8] If Craig Thomson had done his job properly, Lafferty wouldn't have been on the pitch to score.

Even worse was the fact that the second goal was scored by Steven Naismith, who shouldn't even have been playing. It must have stuck in Hibs' craws to see Naismith handed a two-match ban on the very day of the match; a ban that wouldn't affect his featuring against Hibs. Again, if Bobby Madden had done his job properly, then Naismith wouldn't have been on the field of play.

Leaving all that aside, the situation now was that Hibs were three points behind Neo-Gers and would need to win against them by six clear goals in their last game to secure third place. Neo-Gers, meanwhile, only needed a draw against Hibs, assuming Aberdeen lost to Celtic, to finish in second place. It was going to be an interesting last day.

Considering how Hibs had effectively been cheated by two referees, one of whom used to be a season-ticket holder at Ibrox, The People had a bit of a cheek to complain about the referee at Pittordrie; but when has that ever stopped them?

> Referee Steven McLean was awful at Pittodrie, it was never a penalty for Aberdeen's goal as Alfredo Morelos got the ball rather than Kenny McLean.
> Once again a decision has cost my club as it appears whistlers are doing their best to deny us second place.[9]

That was bad enough, but there was worse to come.

> I predict Celtic will let Aberdeen win at the weekend the
> way they did against Hibs to prevent Rangers (sic) finishing
> second.[10]

Talk about paranoid! Another Neo-Gers supporter was rather more philosophical about it.

> Don't be surprised if Celtic play a reserve squad against
> Aberdeen to save their key players for the Scottish Cup
> Final. This surely would give Aberdeen an advantage over
> Rangers (sic) and Hibs in the race for second spot. Most
> clubs would do the same in their situation but it will cause
> serious anger to the supporters of the two other clubs.[11]

Remarkably, it was Celtic that was being put under pressure, even though they had nothing to gain or lose in the final match of the season. And it wasn't just The People exerting this pressure. Gordon Parks joined in a couple of days later, condemning Celtic for not giving their own academy players a chance, which he claimed was to the detriment of Scottish football.[12] (Where was he when Rangers were filling their team with tax-dodging foreigners, I wonder.) Surely, he'd be happy, then, if Celtic put out a youth team against Aberdeen. Something, though, tells me that, somehow, he wouldn't have been.

As it turned out, Celtic put out a strong side, full of first-team regulars. It was either a two-fingered salute to Gordon Parks or a way of saying that they weren't going to lie down. Then again, maybe Brendan Rodgers just wanted to win the last league game of the season, in front of Celtic's own supporters, on the occasion of being presented with the Premiership Champions trophy.

At Easter Road, Hibs managed to go three goals up and it was beginning to look as if they might push Neo-Gers down to that dreaded fourth-place spot. Neo-Gers, however, fought back and, as the match came to a close, were leading 5-4. Another goal from Hibs in injury time meant that both sides had to settle for a draw. The Daily Record called the match a '10-goal epic' but, really, the score emphasised the defensive frailties of both teams.[13]

Nevertheless, it was an exciting and nerve-jangling match for everyone involved. The Hibs supporters' hopes were dashed once Neo-Gers started banging the goals in but, for a brief time, it had

124

looked as if they might finish third. Meanwhile, the Neo-Gers supporters had radios pressed to their ears as they followed what was happening at Celtic Park. The Aberdeen supporters were doing exactly the same, eager for news of what was going on in Edinburgh. That runners-up spot was going right down to the final whistle.

Unfortunately for Neo-Gers, a draw wasn't good enough. In fact, it wouldn't have made any difference even if they had won since Aberdeen managed to hold onto their one-goal lead for practically the whole game.[14] The team was excellent on the day, holding off wave after wave of Celtic attacks and could have taught both Hibs and Neo-Gers a few lessons on how to defend. It had been a gallant effort by Neo-Gers but the league table doesn't lie and Aberdeen had been the better side over the season.

The People, however, were livid, lashing out at everybody. Celtic, of course, got the brunt of it.

> What a fantastic game at Easter Road and a terrific advert for Scottish football. Shame it was all undermined in Glasgow by Celtic not trying a leg against Aberdeen.[15]

> I think it's a conspiracy. Celtic laid down to Dons and they should be investigated for fraud.[16]

> I wonder if Celtic get another trophy for lying down to Aberdeen? As far as I'm concerned they cheated the Scottish league with that performance.[17]

In fact, the match stats for the game at Celtic Park said otherwise. Celtic had 19 shots at goal to Aberdeen's 5, with 6 on target to Aberdeen's 1. Unfortunately, that one shot on target of Aberdeen's resulted in a goal. Celtic also had 8 corners to only 1 for Aberdeen.[18] That certainly didn't sound like a team that wasn't trying.

But Celtic weren't the only ones getting it in the neck. The referees came in for their share of stick as well.

> A stone wall red card and a stone wall penalty not given
> Is it getting to the stage we need to score 5 every game to beat the cheating bastards of referees in this country? How many times are we having to go over this now.

How many calls against us before we rid ourselves of the 'paranoia' brigade and realise there is a vendetta against us in the refereeing body.

Every fucking match were up against it.[19]

Do you think this character, and the others moaning about biased referees would agree that Lafferty should have been sent off against Hibs and that Naismith shouldn't have been playing in the first place? That's extremely doubtful. According to The People, they were the only ones that got poor decisions. Apparently, things evening themselves out over a season was no longer the case.

And so, Steven Gerrard's first task as Neo-Gers manager was going to be trying to guide his team through the qualifiers and into the Europa League proper. He was going to have to do a damn sight better than Boxy had the previous year. As usual, though, everything was going to work out fine, just as it was supposed to have done in 2017. The logic used in determining how well Neo-Gers were going to do in Europe was reminiscent of Spike Milligan's brilliantly insane *Goons* sketch about knowing what time it was.[20]

So, how are you going to ensure that you go further in Europe this year?
We're going to bring in new, better players.

Won't that cost money?
Well, yes.

So, where is that money going to come from?
Well, if we do well in Europe, there's the prize money as well as a share of the television profits.

Right, so how will you ensure that you do well in Europe?
By bringing in new and better players.

How will you fund that?
From the money we get from doing well in Europe.

And so the argument would go, round and round and round. No doubt they've got the plan written on a piece of paper! The simple fact was, though, that they had no money for better players. They were going to have to rely on the usual freebies and cheapies and hope that Gerrard was the miracle worker he had been made out to be.

Gerrard's first signings didn't exactly inspire confidence. Well, it did in The People and the agnivores, but they've proven time and again that they'll swallow any old shite. The truth was that it was business as usual in the Action Man's Heid box.

It was said that Allan McGregor was 'returning to Rangers (sic)'.[21] A whole book could be filled arguing the truth of that; better, though, to concentrate on what kind of signing Neo-Gers were getting. After refusing to sign up for Charles Green's new club, McGregor went to Turkish outfit Beşiktaş, who sold him to Hull City a year later. Hull City were like a yo-yo during the second decade of the 21st Century, being up and down between the Premiership and the Championship.

In 2016, with Hull City ready to take part in the Premiership yet again, McGregor was out injured for months.[22] By January, he was fit again but was loaned out to Cardiff City for the rest of the season. His place as first-choice keeper had, by this time, been taken by Eldin Jakupovic.[23]

By the end of the 2016-17 season, Hull City had been relegated yet again. Jakupovic fled to Leicester City[24] and David Marshall, Hull's other goalkeeper, had picked up an ankle injury.[25] McGregor was back in the frame. He continued to be in goal for the rest of the season, only missing a few games. Remarkably, he was chosen as Hull City's Player of the Year in May 2018.[26]

That POTY award, though, meant that McGregor was simply the best of a bad bunch in a disastrous season. Even though they'd been in the Premiership only twelve months before, Hull City finished a deplorable 18th in the Championship, a whopping fifty points behind the leaders, Wolves.[27]

When Neo-Gers came calling, they were hardly pushing against a locked and barred door. Although they finally made McGregor an offer to extend his contract, it could hardly be said that Hull City moved heaven and earth to hold onto him.[28] He was out of contract and was able to sign up to 'Gerrard's Revolution' without too much fuss.

So, what were Neo-Gers getting? Well, McGregor was now thirty-six, but that was neither here nor there; Craig Gordon, of Celtic, was almost the same age. Gordon, however, had replaced McGregor as

Scotland's number-one keeper, which tended to suggest that the latter was on his way out. McGregor was also coming from a struggling team in the depths of the Championship and had a history of serious injury. We're not talking ligaments here; McGregor had done some major damage to his kidney[29] and his back.[30] He was as big a gamble as Gerrard himself was.

Gerrard had this to say about the signing,

> I am delighted to confirm Allan as my second signing this summer as we continue preparations for next season. He is (a) vastly experienced goalkeeper who we feel can add to the options available to us currently.[31]

Actually, one couldn't help but wonder if those 'options' were still going to be 'available' in the new season. It was hardly beyond the realms of possibility that Neo-Gers were going to try to sell Wes Foderingham, Jak Alnwick, or both. After all, the rest of the dross at Neo-Gers were going to prove difficult, if not impossible, to offload.

As Gerrard said, McGregor was his second signing. His first was Scott Arfield, another freebie, of whom the agnivores expected great things. Arfield's previous club, Burnley, had finished a creditable 7th in the English Premier League; not that Arfield had helped much. His contribution to the campaign had been a grand total of two goals.[32] In fact, he hadn't played that much during the season, notching up only 1,335 minutes in total.[33] That's twenty-two-and-a-quarter hours out of a possible fifty-seven. (And that's just counting ninety minutes for each Premier League game. It doesn't count cup matches etc.)

Obviously, Arfield had ended up being down the pecking order at Burnley and, as you might expect, nobody stood in his way when Neo-Gers turned up.[34] Of course, this was swept under the carpet by the agnivores and Arfield himself was bullish, if not downright baw-heided.

> I think I left as a good player and I'm coming back a far better player. Also mentally and physically. With all the promotions and relegations it can only enhance your career, as well as playing in different systems.
> I'm coming back as a natural leader. When I went down there I was almost like a wee boy.[35]

Since Scott Arfield had decided to grace us all with his presence, he expected others to follow suit. 'Gerrard will definitely attract top players,' he said.[36] Barry Ferguson felt exactly the same, expressing a belief that big names would be drawn by the chance of winning silverware and wouldn't mind taking a drop in salary. According to Ferguson,

> I used to watch the Rangers team that Graeme Souness built picking up trophy after trophy. From as far back as I can remember, I knew that was what I wanted to do when I grew up. It was never a question of money.[37]

Never a question of money? Then why did Rangers need to use an EBT to pay him? Surely, he should have been happy with the paltry amount that was stated on his official contract. The guy doesn't half talk shite sometimes; in fact, all the time. Besides, what he was saying contradicted everything The People and the agnivores had been telling us for years.

How many times have we heard about how poor a league the Scottish Premiership is?[38] We had Gordon Parks and his 'lack of ambition' patter,[39] while Kris Boyd hinted at the same thing when talking about Kieran Tierney.[40] Celtic's achievements are always being put down with the argument there's no competition and the Premiership has become a 'one-horse race'.

Why would star players give up on competing in the 'Best League in the World' to come to a footballing backwater? And, since winning titles, cups and medals with Celtic shows a 'lack of ambition', what makes it any different for a player like Jermain Defoe? Why would he want to win silverware that he's constantly been told his nan could win? But...but...but...Gerrard!

It won't make any difference who's in charge at Neo-Gers. Graeme Souness had two advantages: English clubs were banned from Europe and the Bank of Scotland was financing his 'revolution'. There was money to burn at Rangers in those days, with DOS schemes and the like being employed to make it go even further. The situation at Neo-Gers was totally different. To think that top players were going to take a massive pay-cut to take part in what they believed was an inferior league was sheer fantasy.

Kris Boyd admitted that 'As Brendan Rodgers said earlier this week, money talks in football these days and Tierney will eventually realise his earning potential.'[41] And money was going to talk when it came to Neo-Gers as well; though with the situation as it was at Ibrox, that money was going to be suffering a serious bout of laryngitis.

Meanwhile, the papers were full of the targets that Gerrard was after. Jermain Defoe, Lucas Leiva and Martin Skrtel appeared to be top of the list,[42] although it was doubtful that Neo-Gers could afford to match the wages they were currently getting. Maybe Barry Ferguson would be right, and these characters would decide that they already had more than enough money;[43] one could always hope. A more promising scenario, however, was the Sun's opinion that Defoe might be available on loan, with Bournemouth 'paying a slice of his salary'.[44] That, however, was unlikely, since he'd only joined Bournemouth in the summer of 2017.

Leeds United had been after Kyle Bartley of Swansea City for a while and Bartley himself had made plain that he wanted to leave Swansea at the end of the 2017-18 season, even though there were three years left on his contract. Swansea wanted £5m for the defender but, apparently, Leeds imagined they could get him for half that amount. Neo-Gers, meanwhile, thought they were going to be able to jump in and steal Bartley from under the nose of Leeds.[45]

Bartley, though, had been out of action, on and off, for the best part of a year with a gammy knee.[46] What happened next would determine where he would be playing in 2018-19. If we were to make a full recovery, then Swansea would probably stick to their £5m valuation; after all, they were back in the Championship and would need him or be able to afford a replacement.

If his operations were not, or not completely, successful, Swansea might well cut their losses and drop the price. Leeds would probably pull out, not wanting to pay a couple of million plus wages for a player that was going to spend all his time on the treatment table. Neo-Gers might well end up with him hobbling round Auchenhowie, with the agnivores constantly telling us that he was 'just about ready' to appear on the pitch. Remember, Neo-Gers have a history of making dodgy decisions; Kranjčar springs to mind.

The way things were going to go for Neo-Gers was probably presaged by what happened to the bid they made for Connor Goldson. It was an undisclosed amount and was immediately rejected by Brighton, who felt that it 'fell well below Albion's valuation of the defender'.[47] That begged a rather intriguing question: were Neo-Gers *really* making bids for players that they hoped to sign?

Ever since its inception, Neo-Gers has been surrounded by smoke and mirrors, with Level 5 feeding feel-good stories to the media. It was all very well Neo-Gers making bids, but one couldn't help but suspect that they were deliberately making unrealistically low ones. The agnivores could report on how Neo-Gers 'just missed out on' players and praise Gerrard for his ambition. Meanwhile, The People, gullible as ever, would view all this apparent activity and be willing to hand over their hard-earned for season tickets. By the time they realised what was going on, it would be too late.

The probability was that Gerrard, like Warbs and Boxy before him, wouldn't see out a complete season in the Premiership. Yes, victories against wee, diddy teams in the Europa qualifiers would keep The People onside for a while. (Assuming the team could manage *that* this time round.) And a trip over to Belfast to gub Linfield 10-0 would have the Neo-Gers supporters salivating. Meanwhile, the agnivores would be predicting that Rangers (sic) would be making a clean sweep of all the trophies in the upcoming season and that Gerrard would be manager of the year. We've seen it all before!

<u>13</u>
<u>Real World</u>

While all the orgasmic pronouncements were appearing in the press about what a success Gerrard was going to be and all the stars that would be coming to Ibrox, reality, being the bastard that it is, was closing in to put the kibosh on everything. As usual, we had to rely on bloggers and reading between the lines of the agnivores' pish to get the truth.

For a start, despite the agnivores banging on about Gerrard having a clear-out, there didn't seem to be much movement on that front. Nobody wanted any of the Action Man's Heids, as their uselessness had been paraded in various games for all the world to see. One of them, Bruno Alves, had been picked for Portugal's World Cup squad[1] and everybody at Ibrox would be keeping their fingers crossed that he managed to impress somebody, *anybody*, enough to make a bid. The chances were, though, that he might not even get a game.

Then there was Neo-Gers' star attraction; Alfredo Morelos. The general consensus was that Neo-Gers were going to have to cash in, although he might not be commanding the huge fees that had been reported in January and February. This was especially true since after agreeing 'a new deal two months ago, he has only found the net three times in the Scottish Premiership.'[2] Fortunately for Neo-Gers, there was interest being shown, with Ibrox Noise reporting that he was 'the target for a bunch of clubs with Turkish cracks Besiktas looking for his services.'[3]

Actually, that was just the usual agnivore/People hyperbole; only Besiktas was showing any interest in Morelos. The Turkish club wasn't taking any chances, however, and 'want to sign Morelos on a year-long loan with a view to signing him permanently if he impresses, rather than a permanent move.'[4] And if that's the best anybody could do for Morelos, then it didn't bode well for the rest of the Neo-Gers squad.

The agnivores and The People went on about an 'Ibrox exodus' when, really, the only ones leaving were loan players going back to their home clubs. As for Neo-Gers' permanent players, all we had were rumours and possibilities; not one Action Man's Heid had been offloaded yet. It looked unlikely that any of them would be; unless Neo-Gers were ready to sell them all on at a loss. Even then, it would be touch-and-go.

One player that The People definitely wanted rid of was Michael O'Halloran. He had made the mistake of going to watch the Scottish Cup final and sitting among the Celtic supporters.[5] He had been a youth player at Celtic and his father still worked there as a coach, making The People cast doubt on his allegiances. In fact, there was no evidence of him celebrating and it does seem that he was simply there to watch the game.[6] Such excuses, however, cut no ice with The People.

> It should be said that – despite attempts on social media to portry (sic) it otherwise – Gers fans' anger has nothing to do with O'Halloran's religion (the striker is a Celtic supporting catholic) but everything to do with him sitting in with the Gers' biggest rivals at a cup final.
>
> Hearts fans would be furious if one of their players was pictured supporting Hibs at a cup final, Man United fans would be furious if one of their's (sic) was in with City or Liverpool fans and Arsenal fans would be spitting feathers if Mesut Ozil was spotted in with the Spurs fans.[7]

You wonder, though, if they're right about that kind of intense rivalry. Would supporters *really* be that furious if one of their players was seen among their rivals' fans? O'Halloran, remember, gave no indication whatsoever that he was supporting Celtic. I seem to remember that Danny McGrain was known to nip along to Ibrox and stand among the Rangers supporters when he wasn't playing. Strangely, the only grief he got was from the Rangers supporters around him. It's definitely a *People* thing.

As for the protestations (no pun intended) about it having nothing to do with O'Halloran's religion, those had already been shown to be a load of rubbish. Earlier in May, O'Halloran had visited Holy Family RC Church, Mossend in North Lanarkshire to talk about his time at a Catholic school. This, of course, ended up on the church's Facebook page, prompting all manner of filth from The People.

So Michael O'Halloran had a nice wee scummy t***y pape day oot. That's nice. Fenian b******.[8]

I'm hearing the pedo in robes called him Hun Scum for a wee joke.[9]

Always knew he was a fenian mhanky b****** probably fiddled way bheast.[10]

That second one showed a remarkable lack of awareness of irony, as well as spelling. Those comments certainly put paid to any notion that The People weren't concerned with O'Halloran's religion. Fortunately for them, it already looked like O'Halloran was keen to get out.[11]

If the reported exodus was, in reality, merely a trickle, traffic in the other direction wasn't exactly moving at speed either. It was still early days but, already, targeted players were turning down Neo-Gers in droves. So much for the 'Gerrard Effect'! James McArthur, for example, turned the Ibrox club down flat, saying he wanted to stay at Crystal Palace.[12] Lucas Leiva also seemed rather keen to stay where he was.[13]

Even the man that appeared to be Gerrard's number-one target didn't seem to be interested. Martin Skrtel posted a message on Instagram, backed by Fenerbahce's crest, saying, 'You know what I mean?'[14] Well, it wasn't entirely clear what he meant, but it certainly looked as if he was going to be staying at his current club.

For all the big talk of the agnivores, it didn't look as if Gerrard was the draw that they'd hoped. Possibly, all those 'huge stars' wanted to wait to see how well he did as a manager before throwing their lot in with him. That meant he was going to need time to build a team that would overtake Celtic. Unfortunately, time was something that wasn't allowed at Ibrox; The People demanded instant success.

This knowledge, no doubt, influenced the bookies, who were giving odds of 1/4 that Gerrard wouldn't win a single trophy at Ibrox.[15] Even worse, he was 4/6 to leave before the end of the 2018-19 season and even money to be sacked before the season was over.[16] It could hardly be called a vote of confidence. The People, though, were still bullish; unrealistically so.

With players like Martin Skrtel, John McGinn, Scott Arfield, Allan McGregor, Oli McBurnie, Kyle Bartley, Harry Wilson and Connor Goldson in the Rangers team we should not only be able to mount a challenge to Celtic next season but also make our mark in the Europa League.[17]

Considering that most of those names hadn't signed for Neo-Gers and probably never would, that was serious delusion. But it was hard to blame the Neo-Gers supporters for being over-optimistic since the agnivores were feeding them constant stories about how their team was going to dominate the coming season. Of course, they couldn't keep couching things in those terms without looking totally biased so we were fed the myth that Scotland needed a strong Rangers (sic). It would be good for Celtic too, since more of a challenge would help them do better in Europe, wouldn't it?

This is the way the question was put to Brendan Rodgers, but they didn't quite get the answer they were expecting.

It's not even a conversation. It's not a conversation. Talk about Aberdeen. Aberdeen were second. Derek McInnes has done a brilliant job so you should talk about them.[18]

A strong Aberdeen, however, didn't fit the script the agnivores had been given by Jabba; it was a strong Neo-Gers or nothing. Whatever the agenda behind the question, it was clear that Rodgers wasn't overly concerned about Gerrard's appointment. He certainly didn't come across as somebody that was 'running scared', as The People would have it.

Does the thought of Steven Gerard and the array of talent he's going to attract to Ibrox strike so much fear into the SFA they have to start another witch hunt? It seems every time something positive happens at Rangers (sic) the grim reapers come calling.[19]

The delusion was extremely strong with this one. Not only were Celtic supposed to be afraid but the SFA, since it was obviously run by Peter Lawwell, was scared too. And that 'witch hunt' he was

135

talking about was simply the SFA doing its job as a regulator, albeit seven years too late.

Most of us had forgotten about Resolution 12,[20] but *Auldheid* and others were determined that something was going to be done about Rangers being wrongly given a licence to participate in European football in 2011. Finally, in September 2017, the SFA compliance officer announced that he was looking into the matter.[21]

Of course, it's doubtful if the compliance officer would have bothered if it weren't for the fact that the truth had come out during the Craig Whyte trial. All the stories about Rangers' tax debt being still 'in dispute' had been shown up for the pack of lies they were. It was clear that the compliance officer had no choice but to act and that the SFA would be looking to cover their own arses.

And so it turned out. In May 2018, Neo-Gers were served with a Notice of Complaint that they, being, as they claimed, 'still Rangers', had broken the rules in 2011. A hearing was scheduled for the 26th of June and Neo-Gers had until the 22nd of May to respond.[22] The Ibrox club decided not to wait that long and released yet another statement. With a completely straight face and no sense of irony, Neo-Gers claimed,

> This new Notice of Complaint neglects to properly capture the provisions of prior agreements made between the Club and the SFA.
>
> The Club will fiercely resist this reconstructed Notice of Complaint. Unfortunately, monies that should be available to Scottish youth and grassroots football will be diverted into another rehearsal of seven-year-old debates on the rights and wrongs of events that the SFA should have prevented at a time when doing so would have served a useful purpose.[23]

Presumably, those 'prior agreements' refer to the secret 'Five-Way Agreement', part of which, as far as we know, stipulated that Neo-Gers would be responsible for the footballing debts of Rangers. One would assume that any punishment for wrongdoings on the part of Rangers would come under this heading. The Neo-Gers board, however, obviously disagreed. This was one of those occasions when it suited them to admit they were a new club.

So used to getting their own way was the Neo-Gers board that this Notice of Complaint had come totally from left field. The arguments about money being diverted from people that needed it showed the sheer brass neck of everyone connected with Neo-Gers. The amounts involved were small beer indeed compared with how much Rangers, whose trophies Neo-Gers claimed, had stolen from HMRC.

Given the SFA's previous dealings with Neo-Gers and its attitude of 'moving on' from Rangers' fraudulent activities, it would be a huge surprise if Neo-Gers were to be punished to the fullest extent. More likely would be a token fine, a slap on the wrist and a mild warning not to let it happen again. The problem, however, is that it shines a light on Ibrox finances and how the SFA responds to them.

Neo-Gers had already been granted a licence to participate in Europe; something which the Daily Record couldn't help crowing over. 'So-called experts cast this in doubt due to the finances of the Ibrox club.'[24] Not surprisingly, nobody put their name to this Jabba-fed crap. What wasn't mentioned was the fact that UEFA still had to verify the licence. But that was just a formality, wasn't it?

Actually, it wasn't. With UEFA's reputation for corruption, the organisation was going to have to regain the trust of football supporters throughout Europe. Part of this, obviously, was ensuring that it imposed its own rules fairly and without favour. The first casualty of this new-found integrity was to be AC Milan. UEFA were concerned that the Italian club wasn't sticking to the Financial Fair Play regulations and referred the matter to its adjudicatory panel for a ruling. The concern was over a loan that was due to be paid back in October 2018.[25]

If UEFA was sticking to the rules over one loan, they'd be having a fit if they had a close look at Neo-Gers' finances! The whole club was being run on loans, including the one from Close Brothers. Clubs aren't supposed to spend more than they earn, and yet Neo-Gers consistently post huge losses while still signing players. We would have to wait until the end of May to see what UEFA would make of the shambles at Ibrox. The SFA certainly had cause to worry as they shouldn't have granted Neo-Gers a licence in the first place.

To put more pressure on the SFA, Jabba riffled through his, no doubt copious, folders to see what he could find. Something along the lines of 'Proddy bastards' would have fit the bill perfectly, but

137

those sleekit, Taigy fuckers never came out with their bigotry in public. The best he could do was some unknown member of the SFA board, who had made a comment twelve years ago in an unknown magazine.

Gary Ralston, who had become Jabba's favourite glove puppet, broke the 'news' in the Daily Record. In 2006, Gary Hughes, who was then CEO of publishing firm CMPI, gave an interview to licensed trade magazine, *The Publican*, in which he said,

> The next best thing to being at Celtic Park (only the great unwashed venture South to Ibrox) is watching the game, pint of Tennents in hand along with some like-minded souls.[26]

As comments go, it was pretty anodyne, especially compared to the filth that normally emanates from Ibrox. It's something that any football fan might say about rival supporters; The People, however, decided to exaggerate things just a bit.

The thread on the matter on Rangers (sic) Media was called, 'SFA Bigot Exposed', and some of The People rushed to agree with this heading.

> Donald Findlay had to resign as a director of Rangers after being caught singing a party tune at a Rangers event, this cunt is a confessed scum supporter and obviously a bigot but is supposed to be impartial?[27]

> Scottish footballs hierarchy and it's (sic) decision making quangos are riddled with like-minded bastards. We have little chance of success with these bastards running the show for their beloved catholic institution. Surprised this got to print. Hopefully there is someone with a dossier on all these bastards with their blatant hatred that can get exposed for all to see.[28]

> Holds senior positions in blue chip companies and a prominent postiton in the SFA.
> On the surface he would seem a successful and balanced individual.

138

However scratch the surface and he's yet another Celtic supporting bigot.
Good riddance.[29]

How the hell the comment could be construed as bigoted was a complete mystery. Most of the complainers confined themselves to expressing the view that it was simply offensive. If it was so offensive, however, why didn't somebody complain about it twelve years ago, when the article was published? Well, not everyone would have been able to get their hands on a copy of *The Publican*, but there are plenty of bar owners and managers among The People. Surely the Marshalls, rulers of the Louden Tavern, would have seen it.

The answer to that one is simple. Probably the magazine was sent to every pub free, but the likes of the Marshalls wouldn't have touched it. It would have gone straight into the bin without the protective cellophane even being removed. With the lack of brain cells among The People, any Rangers-supporting bar owner or manager would have looked at the title of the magazine with horror. They probably thought it was something to do with Sinn Fein.

In the present, though, The People jumped on this story like a drowning man clutching a straw. Even those that could see nothing bigoted about it saw it as an opportunity to get rid of all the 'Raynjurz-Haturz' in the SFA.

It is a sad game endightment on society that a 12 year old comment that was clearly meant as banter is raked up and will hopefully cost a man his job. Unfortunately we are in a position where we need to pursue absolutely every avenue like this to try and redress the imbalance in Scottish football. I would normally be dead against something like this being used so long after the fact and when it is obviously a throw away comment but after what happened with Chris Graham, and with the current make up of the SFA board, the ground rules have been laid and we can nothing other than abide by them. Whoever dug it out is doing good work.[30]

Should he be sacked for it? No, its a fairly mild dig from a supporter of our rivals, which is laughable given how

139

their fans got panned worldwide for their abundance of mankieness. It was made at a time when he wasnt in a position of power and I dont really find it offensive to be honest.

Do I want him sacked for it? Yes, fuck them. This is exactly the kind of pedantic shite they have tried to do for years, constantly blowing tiny things like this up for PR spin. Fuck them. In the name of sporting integrity, he must be sacked.[31]

There can't be any confidence in his independence in any future decision making, even if this one comment is more stupid than anything else - he has to go.[32]

So, this character couldn't possibly be independent because he was a Celtic supporter. Strangely, though, it was okay for an ex-Rangers employee, Gordon Smith, to have a senior position at the SFA after accusing it of having an agenda against the Ibrox club.[33] Even worse was the fact that one-time SFA President, Campbell Ogilvie, was the recipient of one of David Murray's EBTs.[34] And yet, we were supposed to accept that these 'People' were impartial!

Lost among all the recriminations was the fact that Hughes was part of the 'move on' brigade, which wanted all the cheating and lying by Rangers swept under the carpet and forgotten about.[35] But this was about one thing and one thing only: the investigation by the SFA's compliance officer into that UEFA licence in 2011. It was practically a blackmail note: leave us alone or we'll see what else we can dig up.

It might well have worked, if it hadn't been for Honest Dave sticking his crooked nose into the affair. The very same day that the story appeared in the Daily Record, King issued a statement, calling for Hughes to be suspended and a full-scale investigation to be started.[36] This single act turned things around completely.

If King had left well enough alone, the agnivores would have been happy to put pressure on the SFA and would have been ready to point the finger and scream 'hypocrisy' if there were to be any punishment for Neo-Gers over what happened in 2011. Now, however, Honest Dave had made things official and had put it out there that Neo-Gers wanted punishments handed out for something that had happened in the past. Since they were pretending to be 'still Rangers', it left them without a leg to stand on. The SFA, by Neo-Gers own admission, would be perfectly justified in continuing the investigation into the events of 2011. Whether anything would come of it or not was another matter entirely.

While King was in 'petty' mode, he had yet another statement to make. On the Neo-Gers website, he thanked The People for renewing their season tickets and told of a huge waiting list for first-time buyers. He spoke of putting Neo-Gers supporters first and his regret that

> An unfortunate consequence of putting our supporters first is that this increased demand negatively impacts on the number of tickets which will be allocated to visiting teams. This means all visiting fans will now be situated in the corner between the Broomloan and Sandy Jardine Stands.[37]

This meant that Celtic's allocation was going to be reduced from 7000 tickets to a mere 800. Barry Ferguson claimed that this made economic sense, giving Steven Gerrard some much-needed extra funds. He said,

> The bottom line as to why Rangers will now look to sell 7,000 more season books is that it will significantly increase revenue this summer.
> I'd imagine the cost of a season ticket is just over £350 so by my reckoning that's almost £2.5m in extra revenue, so it makes perfect sense to do that.[38]

Gordon Waddell came to the same conclusion as Barry Ferguson, even suggesting the same couple of million extra income. He, however, was critical of the move, seeing it as short-sighted.

> It's about money, and how they can get their hands on more of it now. Not tomorrow, not at New Year, not after the split. Now.[39]

Both these characters, however, were overlooking one, important point: those seats in the Broomloan Stand weren't left lying empty all season, waiting for the arrival of the Celtic supporters. The standard practice with season tickets at Ibrox has always been that ones for the Broomloan Stand have been cheaper because they don't include Celtic matches. Celtic has done the exact same thing for the seats allocated to Rangers/Neo-Gers supporters. The point is that season tickets for the Broomloan would have been sold whether or not the purchasers would have to move when Celtic came calling. The up-front money made by cutting Celtic's allocation would be nowhere near £2m.

Last season, Celtic supporters were charged £49 for a seat in the Broomloan. Let's round that up to £50, which is reasonable since the price would be increasing for next season. With Celtic supporters getting 6,200 less tickets, that means Neo-Gers missing out on two paydays of over £300,000. It's doubtful that the Broomloan season tickets will be £100 dearer than they would have been but, even if we allow that, it means only £600,000 extra coming in earlier. In reality, though, it's going to be a lot less than that.

Supporters that wangled themselves child tickets rather than pay Third Division prices (Remember that?) weren't going to be too happy to stump up an extra ton just to stop Celtic supporters getting their arses into the Broomloan. Besides, the Broomloan housed what Neo-Gers called their 'Family Section'. It had made sense to give up those particular seats to the Celtic support; after all, they didn't want the children being terrified by the sight of an Irish flag! Now, though, with Celtic's allocation drastically reduced, that fear was diminished accordingly. And how much flag-waving could the Celtic supporters do with vaping devices embedded in their skulls?

The point is that, with the Broomloan full of weans, even less cash would be coming in. Neo-Gers would be fortunate to even recoup half of the £600,000 being given up by cutting Celtic's allocation. Whatever the amount raised, it certainly wouldn't constitute any kind of warchest and it certainly scotched any talk of King looking to get extra money in early.

Since the reduction in Celtic's seat allocation is nothing to do with finance, then the only reason it's being done is to suck up to The People. Cutting the number of Celtic supporters at Ibrox has long been something that The People have called for; as we saw in Chapter 4, it was even raised at the AGM. They were overjoyed at the news.

Fucking fantastic news![40]

142

Huge critic of the board but fair play for that and like that it's been done as a well deserved thank you to the fans.
Brilliant Rangers (sic).[41]

Have I woke up in some weird alternative universe.
Get in the Rangers (sic) board.[42]

The same approving noises were made regarding Dave King's demand for an investigation into Gary Hughes.

Fair to say that this appears to signal a new approach from Rangers (sic) in their dealings with the football authorities and a number of the clubs in Celtic's SFA and SPFL cabal who have run Scottish football into the ground. Expect more to come on that front very soon.[43]

This obvious pandering to The People, even to the detriment of Neo-Gers' finances and reputation, could only mean one thing: there was bad news coming down the pike. Looked at from that angle, Honest Dave's interference in the Gary Hughes business maybe wasn't as stupid as first appeared. But what could that bad news be? Administration? The selling of Ibrox? Actually, it was probably something more mundane, but The People would be suffering just as much.

There had already been bad news on the signings front. The attempt to bring Martin Skrtel to Ibrox had descended into complete farce. When it finally looked like Skrtel wouldn't be leaving Fenerbahce, Jabba's puppet at the Evening Times, Chris Graham, ran with a 'sour grapes' article.

Steven Gerrard is not pursuing a move to bring former Liverpool team-mate Martin Skrtel to Ibrox.
It is understood that the defender is not on the list of potential recruits that Rangers (sic) are targeting this summer as boss Gerrard looks to overhaul his squad ahead of the Europa League qualifiers and new Premiership campaign.[44]

143

That 'never wanted him anyway' reaction was reminiscent of the way Neo-Gers had responded to the knock-back from Derek McInnes. It was pathetic and soon shown to be untrue. To the embarrassment of Neo-Gers, Skrtel's agent appeared on Slovakian TV, insisting that he'd been in contact with Gerrard. Apparently the Ibrox club *did* want Skrtel, but simply couldn't afford him.[45]

How many more rebuffs would Neo-Gers receive? Assuming, of course, that the bids they were making were real ones and not just to make The People believe that their club was serious about mounting a challenge to Celtic. As prospective deal after prospective deal fell apart and nobody arrived at Ibrox except a couple more Action Man's Heids, moves would have to be made to keep The People onside. As the comment above said, regarding King 'standing up' to the SFA, we could 'Expect more to come on that front very soon.'

14
Everybody's Happy Nowadays

On the 26th of May, Steven Gerrard was in Kiev to watch his old team take on Real Madrid in the Champions League final. A couple of howlers from the Liverpool goalie and a wonder strike from Gareth Bale led to the Spanish team winning 3-1. As he watched these two European heavyweights play, surely Gerrard must have been wondering what he'd let himself in for at Neo-Gers.

Liverpool have won five European Cups, two Cup-Winners Cups, one UEFA Cup and three Super Cups. Real Madrid, meanwhile, have won thirteen European Cups, two Cup-Winners Cups, four Super Cups, three Intercontinental Cups and four Club World Cups. After mingling in such heady company, Gerrard was on his way home to take charge of a six-year-old club that claimed to be the 'most successful club in the world', even though it had won nothing more prestigious than a Petrofac Cup.

He would have already visited the Ibrox Trophy Room and been amazed that many of the items on display weren't trophies at all. Most of them had been gifts to Rangers, including the St. Etienne Bike, a golden football and even the famous Loving Cup.[1] It would have been like standing in his granny's living room, with the display cabinet showing all the holiday souvenirs brought back by various members of the family.

Gerrard would be buoyed, though, by the rapturous reception he'd received from The People. You can't help but wonder if he had looked back to find out about how the same welcome had been accorded Boxy, Warbs and, when Rangers were still alive, Paul Le Guen. Had he seen the way things had ended with those men? Was he aware that, to The People, second place in the league was considered abject failure? And did he know that if he were to be sacked prematurely he'd have to go to court to get the money he was owed? He obviously hadn't paid any attention

145

whatsoever to these matters; otherwise he wouldn't have taken the job.

Quite a few folk have commented on how Gerrard isn't the brightest light on the Christmas tree; in fact, it seems it would be a toss up to find the thickest bloke at Ibrox, Gerrard or John Greig. He's signed a four-year contract but obviously doesn't realise that no manager is at Ibrox for the long haul. He's got one season to overtake Celtic, and that's it. Fail to do that and his arse will be out the door before he's even booked his holidays for summer 2019.

As Phil Mac Giolla Bhain pointed out, the summer close season is The People's favourite time of the year.[2] They can fantasise about all the star players they're going to sign, what they're going to do to Celtic, all the money they're going to make in Europe and how they're going to celebrate '55'. They're like a child, on the run-up to Christmas, dreaming of all the presents they're going to get, only to find that they're *The Little Boy that Santa Claus Forgot*!

Still, they're happy at the moment. The sun's shining, orange Neo-Gers tops will soon be available in markets and dodgy shops, marching season's coming up and Nestlé have brought out tubes that only contain orange Smarties.[3] Life couldn't be better.

Of course, as we all know, trouble is simmering away under the surface at Neo-Gers. Honest Dave appears to have faced down the Takeover Panel and won, but the Financial Authorities can't afford to let this pass. If King is allowed to go his own, merry way, then the rules governing how businesses are run mean nothing. There can only be one winner in this battle and, despite King's bluster, Neo-Gers are eventually going to end up struggling to do business.

If Phil Mac Giolla Bhain is to be believed, then there are already major splits in the Ibrox Board Room and King is becoming increasingly isolated.[4] The fact that Paul Murray and Barry Scott have already flown the coop would suggest that Phil's right. How long will it be before we see another gang of 'Requisitioners'?

And then there's the Big Lie, which has caused no end of problems for the new club and continues to do so. That Notice of Complaint from the SFA regarding the UEFA licence in 2011 wouldn't have gone anywhere near Ibrox if Neo-Gers weren't pretending to be 'still Rangers'. As things stand, they're going to have to answer for that particular bit of cheating. King, with his grandstanding to The People over Gary Hughes, has probably made himself a few enemies at Hampden, as well as admitting that historic wrongdoing should be punished. This isn't going to end well.

Those EBTs, too, are coming back to haunt Neo-Gers. The Tax Man is going after all the recipients and is looking to recoup £24m. They all had until the 31st of May to either pay up or come up with some kind of settlement deal. And, just in case any of The People started bleating about other teams' players using tax-dodging schemes, the Daily Record pointed out that

> HMRC are also targeting users of "disguised renumeration tax avoidance schemes" in thousands of other businesses.[5]

Not everybody had the foresight of Barry Ferguson, or, rather, his advisers, to make sure everything went into his wife's name at the first sign of everything going tits-up.[6] Then again, footballers' marriages and relationships are notoriously fickle, and it would be a brave man indeed that handed over everything to a WAG, leaving himself with nothing if things turned nasty.

For the EBT brigade, however, there was a small glimmer of light at the end of the tunnel. The side contracts the players had with Rangers stipulated that, if the Tax Man came calling, The Club would take care of everything.[7] Nothing was said about holding companies, engine-room subsidiaries or the like; it was *the club* that was underwriting the 'loans'. And, since Neo-Gers claim to be still that self-same club, then, surely, they are liable. All it would take is one brave individual to get his solicitor onto it. I suppose it depends which is more important: money or the love of The People.

Speaking of money, an article appeared in the Daily Record, telling how Steven Gerrard and Gary McAllister were looking at flats in the West End of Glasgow. Apparently, these flats, in a new development, are selling for around £575,000.[8] This could end up being an expensive waste of money. New-builds are notorious for not appreciating much in value, especially in the current climate and Gerrard and McAllister might have to sell in a hurry. Then again, they might be renting, which would be a far more sensible solution. An even better idea would have been to get in touch with Boxy about renting a caravan.

For all we laugh at how thick Gerrard is, there's something about his living arrangements that suggest he might well have his head screwed on properly. It seems that his wife and kids are remaining in England while he works at Neo-Gers. Now, that kind of arrangement is not one that you'd want to last for four years, so, perhaps Gerrard realises that he won't be in Glasgow anywhere near that length of time.

If The People were happy and content with how they saw things panning out next season, some of the agnivores were decidedly not. The big problem for them was the cuts in ticket allocations at Ibrox and Celtic Park. It certainly looked as though Celtic were going to reciprocate Neo-Gers' huge cut in Celtic supporters at their ground.[9] This would probably save Celtic quite a bit of money as the toilets would be less likely to be trashed.

The agnivores, however, bemoaned the loss of 'atmosphere'. Gordon Waddell summed up the general feeling of those in the media:

> Rangers (sic) and Celtic have none of the best players in the world, rounded to the nearest zero. The game's notoriety, its infamy, its legend, is built entirely on its blood-curdling mayhem.
> Take that away and what are you left with?[10]

Gordon Parks agreed completely.

> Any claim the Old Firm (sic) had on their derby being the world's best has never been based on the calibre of football on the pitch.
> It has always been about the madness and mayhem which comes pouring from the stands.
> Let's be blunt - it's the full-blooded nastiness which takes the breath away and makes this match so special.[11]

Some supporters felt the same way and one called the Daily Record Hotline to no doubt speak for many,

> BT Sport and SKY will pull the plug on Scottish football if the ticket cuts go ahead as planned.
>
> Our unique selling point is the Glasgow derby and if you reduce Celtic 's allocation from 8,000 to 800 at Ibrox and vice-versa with the Rangers (sic) fans at Celtic Park then it just won't be the same.
>
> The TV companies will do walking away if there is not a major rethink on this issue.[12]

BT and Sky couldn't give a monkey's toss about Scottish football; their main concern is selling a product to an English audience, which outnumbers the Scottish one by more than 1000%. Essentially, what all these agnivores and punters were saying is that Scottish football, even the Celtic vs Neo-Gers Derby, simply isn't good enough for an English audience. How could our football even hope to compete with the 'Greatest league in the world'? English folk don't want to watch a Glasgow Derby for the football; they want blood.

What the agnivores were admitting was that it was all the bile and bigotry that was the draw. English folk couldn't care less who was on the pitch; as far as they were concerned you could just hand weapons to all the supporters and let them kill each other. Basically, what Scottish football was selling to England was a version of *The Hunger Games* for the entertainment of our overlords. You can just imagine the sneering faces in London as they laugh, 'Cor bloimey! Look at the Sweaty Socks! Wot're they loike, eh?'

I remember once hearing the comedian Dara Ó Briain refer to Glasgow as 'Belfast Lite' and it's quite shocking to think that's the way the world sees our largest city. Even more shocking, however, is the admission that our football authorities are relying on this perception to bring money into the game. Suddenly, though, a lot of things make sense that didn't before.

It's always been a puzzle how it's made out that Celtic supporters are just as bigoted as those of Neo-Gers when it's clearly not the case. The assumption has always been that everyone's too afraid to call out The People. Now, however, we can see that the whole matter is being cynically manipulated to sell the Glasgow Derby to England. What's the point of selling a one-sided verbal battle? Everyone outside of Scotland has to believe that 'both sides are as

149

bad as each other' to make the thing a viable product. It doesn't matter that there's no evidence of Celtic supporters being bigoted; the important thing is that folk *believe* that they are.

Part of the 'enjoyment' of the spectacle is for the audience to feel superior to the ones they're watching. There's no point if that audience believes that only one side is full of bigots; the danger there is that they might see Celtic as morally superior and lose their whole reason for watching. They have to believe that *all* Scottish folk behave like that; not just certain sections. Our media certainly pander to this delusion.

Another media obsession that suddenly makes sense is the constant harping on about the need for a strong Neo-Gers; a 'strong Rangers', as the agnivores would have it. It's always been a confusing issue: why do we have to have a strong *Neo-Gers* for a competitive league? Why not a strong Aberdeen or a strong Hibs, or any other team, for that matter? Now we can see that the argument has nothing whatsoever to do with 'competitive leagues'. The fact is that no other Scottish team can be relied upon to pour out ninety minutes of pure hatred. And that, apparently, is what the audience wants.

The problem with marketing the Glasgow Derby at present is that the voices that provide the much-vaunted 'atmosphere' have been quietened. Seeing their team utterly outclassed on the pitch means that the Ibrox Choir mainly sit in stunned silence these days. The People then tend to sneak out long before the match is finished. There's no point in their songs of triumphalism and hatred when they know that their team is shite.

And that's where the constant cries for a strong Neo-Gers come in. If it were possible, the agnivores would be shouting for the Scottish Government to pour money into Ibrox so that the team could mount a serious challenge to Celtic. It's essential to give The People something to sing about. After all, BT and Sky will just abandon Scottish football if they can't provide at least four bigot-fests a year. That seems to be the standard opinion among the agnivores and our football authorities at any rate.

The fear among the agnivores, though, is that not all members of the SFA and SPFL boards share this vision. They have consequently taken it upon themselves to do something about it. What seemed to have started out as a bit of petty grandstanding by

King and his creatures in the media is rapidly turning into an attempt at some kind of Stalinist purge.

It was only a couple of days after the manufactured outrage over Gary Hughes that a member of the SPFL board came under attack. The story was that SPFL Chairman, Murdoch MacLennan, had taken up a post as a non-executive director of 'Dublin based Independent News and Media PLC - an Irish media giant which is part owned by Desmond and his long-term associate Denis O'Brien.'[13] The SPFL insisted that there was no conflict of interest, but it was clear from the Daily Record's article that the agnivores believed there was.

No sooner had the story emerged than Honest Dave appeared with another statement. He called for McLennan to be suspended and for a full investigation to be carried out. With breath-taking audacity, he said,

> It is equally important that any conflicts of interest, or even the perception of such, whereby positions within the Scottish football authorities could be undermined, or abused, must be aggressively rooted out of our game.[14]

The People were a lot less circumspect in what they were saying.

> When ppl like this are in power we can see why the agenda against our club has been so bad trying to destroy us and holding us back from any success with only negative stuff allowed.[15]

> Get that rabid bastard to fuck.
> Time for King to call for this scummy bastards's head.[16]

> We need to keep hounding these taigs out!.... media pressure and PR from our club is required consistently to highlight these cunts... they are so full of hatred and thick as fuck that they will trip themselves up at every turn due to their poor segregated education system....[17]

These dirty, rotten, stinking, bead rattling, nappy ripping, fenian bastards are running everything here now.

Just like the magic carpet men are doing in England.

We'll soon have Mozzie Kathliks in positions of importance![18]

As you can see, King, Jabba and the agnivores are stirring up some dangerous emotions with this business; God knows what they think the outcome will be. It certainly betrays the sheer hypocrisy of all of them. Nobody had a thing to say when individuals with EBTs from Rangers were sitting in positions of authority. In fact, the attitudes of the football authorities, the agnivores, The People and Neo-Gers made the situation appear even worse.

To all these groups and individuals, the EBTs are, and always have been, viewed as loans and nothing more. Despite the judgments of various courts to the contrary, this opinion still seems to prevail. This, of course, begs the question as to who is more compromised: someone that happens to be on the board of a company in which Dermot Desmond has shares or the likes of Campbell Ogilvie, who owed money to Oldco Rangers? As King himself said, even the 'perception' should have had alarm bells ringing.

It's clear, though, that just like The People's calls for an investigation into the sexual abuse of children in Scottish football, King doesn't want any wide-ranging enquiry. All that matters is getting at Celtic, even if that means feeding the dangerous paranoias of The People.

Remember that character, quoted in the last chapter, who said, 'Expect more to come on that front very soon'? Obviously, he was right. And what's more, this was probably going to be a major feature of the 2018-19 season. Every defeat suffered by Neo-Gers will be blamed on 'malevolent forces' within the SFA and SPFL. In fact, even failure in Europe will lead to claims of some of *them* having taken over UEFA.

Anyway, here's to another season and another treble for Celtic. Nobody in their right mind can see any kind of challenge coming from the Ibrox Action Man's Heids, no matter who's in charge.

This time next year Gerrard will have been run out of Govan, yet another casualty of the Big Lie. Here's hoping that, in the time between now and then, he's as entertaining as Boxy. It's a hard act to follow, but I'm sure Gerrard's up to the task.

NOTES

INTRODUCTION

[1] https://www.dailyrecord.co.uk/sport/football/football-news/new-rangers-signing-bruno-alves-10535948

[2]https://www.dailyrecord.co.uk/sport/football/football-transfer-news/rangers-complete-bruno-alves-signing-10532875

[3] https://www.bbc.co.uk/sport/football/40187603

[4] https://www.bbc.co.uk/sport/football/40240221

[5]https://philmacgiollabhain.ie/2018/05/21/a-bright-reality-and-dark-fantasies/

[6] https://www.bbc.co.uk/sport/football/40410727

[7]https://twitter.com/GaryLineker/status/882332468870819841?ref_src=twsrc%5Etfw&ref_url=
https%3A%2F%2Fextra.ie%2F2017%2F07%2F05%2Fsport%2Fsoccernews%2Frangers-out-of-europe&tfw_site=ExtraIRL

[8]https://twitter.com/paddypower/status/882330618692071425?ref_src=twsrc%5Etfw&ref_url=
https%3A%2F%2Fextra.ie%2F2017%2F07%2F05%2Fsport%2Fsoccernews%2Frangers-out-of-europe&tfw_site=ExtraIRL

[9] https://www.thescottishsun.co.uk/sport/football/1241298/pedro-caixinha-apologises-to-rangers-fans-whilst-standing-in-the-middle-of-a-bush-after-humiliating-euro-exit-to-progres-niederkorn/

[10]http://www.eveningtimes.co.uk/news/15390918.Video__%20Furious_Rangers_fans_block_team_bus_and_
shout_abuse_following_Europa_League_exit_in_Luxembourg/?ref=ar

[11]https://www.dailyrecord.co.uk/sport/football/football-news/scottish-footballs-most-shameful-european-10741096

[12] https://www.bbc.co.uk/sport/football/40766961

[13]http://www.talkingbaws.com/2017/08/video-camera-angle-show-john-beaton-sent-ryan-jack-off/

[14]https://www.dailyrecord.co.uk/sport/football/football-news/sfa-confirm-rangers-appeal-ryan-10987136

[15]https://www.change.org/p/scottish-football-association-end-the-anti-rangers-views-amongst-referees-in-scotland

Chapter 1

[1] www.bbc.co.uk/sport/football/41895487

[2] http://forum.rangersmedia.co.uk/topic/310002-todays-scum-result/

[3] https://www.change.org/p/uefa-ban-celtic-from-the-champions-league

[4] http://www.vanguardbears.co.uk/article.php?i=165&a=fight-fire-with-fire
[5] https://www.bbc.co.uk/sport/football/41196748
[6] https://www.bbc.co.uk/sport/football/41328904
[7] https://www.followfollow.com/forum/threads/rangers-v-celtic-match-thread-sky-sports.3381/
[8] www.eveningtimes.co.uk/sport/rangers/15550567.Rangers_boss_Pedro_Caixinha_welcomes_a_different_ chase_at_Ibrox_ahead_of_Celtic_clash/
[9] http://forum.rangersmedia.co.uk/topic/310506-scottish-club-win-v-psg
[10] https://www.bbc.co.uk/sport/football/41290216
[11] https://www.dailyrecord.co.uk/sport/football/football-match-reports/rangers-0-celtic-2-brendan-11223459
[12] https://www.bbc.co.uk/sport/football/41290216
[13] https://www.youtube.com/watch?v=iKijRLCzAdw
[14] https://videocelts.com/2017/09/blogs/fans/how-the-celtic-support-owned-ibrox/
[15] https://www.followfollow.com/forum/threads/that-banner-disgrace-club-have-questions-to-answer.3639/
[16] https://www.youtube.com/watch?v=5zDDFCejuCl
[17] https://www.footballinsider247.com/celtic-demand-inquiry-rangers/
[18] www.bbc.co.uk/news/av/uk-scotland-40506489/supreme-court-finds-in-favour-of-hmrc-in-rangers-big-tax-case
[19] https://www.dailyrecord.co.uk/sport/football/peter-lawwells-mission-expose-scottish-11146603
[20] https://www.dailyrecord.co.uk/sport/football/football-news/stewart-regan-full-qa-opens-11150752
[21] ibid
[22] https://www.scotsman.com/sport/football/competitions/premiership/opinion-stephen-mcilkenny-on-why-sfa-review-is-necessary-for-real-change-1-4561256
[23] https://www.dailyrecord.co.uk/sport/football/football-news/spfl-chief-faces-grilling-over-11174324
[24] https://www.scotsman.com/sport/football/competitions/premiership/rangers-send-angry-letter-to-sfa-over-ebt-call-reports-1-4561440
[25] www.eveningtimes.co.uk/sport/rangers/15551519.Rangers_and_Celtic_on_collision_course_for_Betfred_Cup_ final_following_semi_final_draw/
[26] https://www.bbc.co.uk/sport/football/41450426
[27] https://www.bbc.co.uk/sport/football/41520868
[28] https://www.dailyrecord.co.uk/sport/football/st-johnstone-0-rangers-3-11339300
[29] https://www.bbc.co.uk/sport/football/41520868

[30]https://philmacgiollabhain.ie/2017/07/20/one-big-unhappy-family/#more-9971
[31] ibid
[32]https://philmacgiollabhain.ie/2017/09/29/when-the-barking-dogs-are-inside-the-caravan/#more-10293
[33]https://www.dailyrecord.co.uk/sport/football/football-news/rangers-boss-pedro-caixinha-insists-11383769
[34] ibid
[35] ibid
[36]www.heraldscotland.com/sport/15610840.Pedro_Caixinha_craves_glory_at_Rangers_like_a_vampire_craves_ blood/
[37]https://www.dailyrecord.co.uk/opinion/sport/rangers-lurching-back-dark-desperate-11391073
[38]https://www.dailyrecord.co.uk/sport/football/football-news/rangers-defender-bruno-alves-blasts-11391230
[39]https://www.dailyrecord.co.uk/sport/football/football-news/raging-rangers-slam-sfa-decision-11402076
[40] https://www.dailyrecord.co.uk/sport/football/football-news/motherwells-ryan-bowman-escapes-punishment-11401373
[41] https://rangers.co.uk/news/match-report/rangers-0-2-motherwell/
[42]https://www.dailyrecord.co.uk/sport/football/football-news/pedro-caixinha-qa-rangers-boss-11396110
[43] ibid
[44] ibid
[45]https://www.dailyrecord.co.uk/opinion/sport/hotline/rangers-boss-pedro-caixinha-embarrassment-11390873
[46] https://www.dailyrecord.co.uk/opinion/sport/rangers-lurching-back-dark-desperate-11391073
[47]https://www.thescottishsun.co.uk/sport/football/1735492/rangers-kenny-miller-dave-king-betfred-cup-motherwell/
[48]https://www.thescottishsun.co.uk/sport/football/1751733/pedro-caixinha-vows-to-fight-on-rangers-kilmarnock-1-1-ibrox/
[49] https://www.bbc.co.uk/sport/football/41661422
[50]www.eveningtimes.co.uk/news/15619457.Pedro_Caixinha_s_plea_to_Rangers_fans_after_Kilmarnock_draw__ Stand_by_me/
[51]https://www.dailyrecord.co.uk/sport/football/football-news/pedro-caixinhas-rangers-rebuild-unfit-11410477
[52]https://stv.tv/sport/football/1400805-rangers-call-board-meeting-to-discuss-caixinha-s-future/
[53]https://www.dailyrecord.co.uk/sport/football/football-news/rangers-sack-

pedro-caixinha-after-11413476
[54] ibid
[55] http://news.bbc.co.uk/sport1/hi/football/teams/r/rangers/4758549.stm
[56] https://www.dailyrecord.co.uk/sport/football/football-news/former-rangers-boss-pedro-caixinha-12123600

Chapter 2

[1] https://www.bbc.co.uk/sport/football/39170663
[2] https://www.dailyrecord.co.uk/sport/football/football-news/9-runners-riders-rangers-job-11394074
[3] www.heraldscotland.com/news/15626854.Aberdeen_to_let_Rangers_speak_to_Derek_McInnes___if_
Ibrox_club_agrees_to_pay___1_5m_compensation/
[4] ibid
[5] https://www.dailyrecord.co.uk/sport/football/football-news/john-brown-back-rangers-mark-11436285
[6] ibid
[7] www.bbc.co.uk/sport/football/42104930
[8] ibid
[9] https://www.dailyrecord.co.uk/sport/football/football-news/five-key-points-rangers-agm-11614093
[10] https://rangers.co.uk/news/headlines/king-search-manager/
[11] https://www.bbc.co.uk/sport/football/41703759
[12] https://www.bbc.co.uk/sport/football/41895487
[13] https://www.dailyrecord.co.uk/sport/football/football-news/derek-mcinnes-quit-aberdeen-rangers-11646679
[14] ibid
[15] https://www.afc.co.uk/2017/12/07/business-usual-management-team-elect-stay/
[16] https://rangers.co.uk/news/headlines/club-statement-83/
[17] www.bbc.co.uk/sport/football/42284211
[18] ibid
[19] ibid
[20] https://www.dailyrecord.co.uk/sport/football/football-news/derek-mcinnes-turned-down-rangers-11658289
[21] https://philmacgiollabhain.ie/2017/12/07/the-formation-of-doubts-about-sevco/#more-10624
[22] https://www.dailystar.co.uk/sport/football/661542/New-Rangers-manager-Derek-McInnes-problem-Jonatan-Johansson-Graeme-Murty

[23]https://philmacgiollabhain.ie/2017/12/07/the-formation-of-doubts-about-sevco/#more-10624
[24] https://rangers.co.uk/news/headlines/club-statement-graeme-murty/
[25]https://www.dailyrecord.co.uk/sport/football/football-news/rangers-appoint-graeme-murty-manager-11737739
[26] https://www.bbc.co.uk/sport/football/42075928
[27] https://www.bbc.co.uk/sport/football/42126636
[28] https://www.bbc.co.uk/sport/football/42295945
[29] https://www.bbc.co.uk/sport/football/42244866
[30] https://www.bbc.co.uk/sport/football/42290487
[31] https://www.bbc.co.uk/sport/football/42375784
[32] www.bbc.co.uk/sport/football/42463667
[33] https://rangers.co.uk/news/match-report/celtic-0-0-rangers-3/
[34]https://www.dailyrecord.co.uk/sport/football/football-match-reports/celtic-0-rangers-0-graeme-11770944

Chapter 3

[1]www.eveningtimes.co.uk/news/15530582.Rangers_to_play_Benfica_in_Eusebio_Cup_clash/
[2] https://www.dailyrecord.co.uk/sport/football/football-news/rangers-fans-blamed-eusebio-cup-11279072
[3] https://www.footballinsider247.com/eusebio-cup-apologise-rangers/
[4] https://www.dailyrecord.co.uk/sport/football/football-news/rangers-play-morton-after-eusebio-11287266
[5] https://en.wikipedia.org/wiki/2017–18_Rangers_F.C._season
[6]https://www.dailyrecord.co.uk/sport/football/football-news/rangers-florida-cup-fixtures-revealed-11314254
[7] https://www.facebook.com/pg/FLCup/about/?ref=page_internal
[8] http://www.floridacup.com/teams
[9]https://www.dailyrecord.co.uk/sport/football/football-news/rangers-florida-cup-fixtures-revealed-11314254
[10] www.floridacup.com/matches
[11]https://www.dailyrecord.co.uk/sport/football/football-news/rangers-atletico-mineiro-florida-cup-11790088
[12] https://rangers.co.uk/matches/atletico-miniero-vs-rangers-110118/
[13]https://www.dailyrecord.co.uk/sport/football/football-match-reports/rangers-1-atletico-mineiro-0-11838609
[14]https://www.dailyrecord.co.uk/sport/football/football-match-reports/rangers-4-corinthians-2-alfredo-11847723

[15]https://www.dailyrecord.co.uk/sport/football/football-match-reports/rangers-1-atletico-mineiro-0-11838609

[16]https://www.dailyrecord.co.uk/sport/football/football-match-reports/rangers-4-corinthians-2-alfredo-11847723

[17]https://www.dailyrecord.co.uk/sport/football/football-news/rangers-vs-corinthians-live-score-11844293

[18] ibid

[19]https://www.dailyrecord.co.uk/sport/football/football-match-reports/rangers-4-corinthians-2-alfredo-11847723

[20]https://www.thescottishsun.co.uk/sport/football/1630914/rangers-mickey-mouse-trophy-florida-cup/

[21] https://rangers.co.uk/matches/atletico-miniero-vs-rangers-110118/

[22]https://www.dailyrecord.co.uk/sport/football/football-match-reports/rangers-1-atletico-mineiro-0-11838609

[23] https://www.dailyrecord.co.uk/all-about/florida-cup

[24]https://www.followfollow.com/forum/threads/so-……did-we-win-the-florida-cup.16174/

[25]www.eveningtimes.co.uk/news/15826485._Fenian_blood___Rangers_fans_belt_out_sectarian__Billy_Boys__ song_in_official_Florida_Cup_video/

[26]https://www.thescottishsun.co.uk/news/2088075/billy-boys-rangers-florida-nil-by-mouth-usa-orlando-video-chant/

[27]https://www.thescottishsun.co.uk/news/2090572/rangers-fans-florida-cup-billy-boys-sectarian-chant-tv-presenter-fabio-brazza/

[28] https://www.thescottishsun.co.uk/news/2087625/rangers-fans-billy-boys-fenian-blood-song-florida-cup-video-tv-presenter-dancing/

[29]https://www.thescottishsun.co.uk/news/2090572/rangers-fans-florida-cup-billy-boys-sectarian-chant-tv-presenter-fabio-brazza/

[30]https://www.followfollow.com/forum/threads/evening-times-reporting-that-the-sectarian-billy-boys-was-sung-in-florida.15936/

[31] ibid

[32] ibid

[33] ibid

[34]https://www.followfollow.com/forum/threads/offensive-behaviour-at-football-act.16462/

[35]https://www.dailyrecord.co.uk/sport/football/football-news/rangers-florida-trip-great-team-11852514

Chapter 4

[1] https://www.dailyrecord.co.uk/sport/football/football-news/rangers-sack-

pedro-caixinha-after-11413476

[2]https://philmacgiollabhain.ie/2017/12/13/preparing-to-open-the-austerity-window-at-sevco/

[3]www.heraldscotland.com/news/15223755.Rangers_chairman_Dave_King_faces_legal_action_after_defying_ takeover_ruling/

[4] https://twitter.com/BBCAlLamont/status/918478786492026881

[5] https://twitter.com/BBCAlLamont/status/918478591859527680

[6]https://philmacgiollabhain.ie/2017/10/13/impecuniosity-and-credulity/#more-10337

[7]www.eveningtimes.co.uk/sport/13276841.Dave_King____50m_needed_for_Rangers_to_match_Celtic/

[8] https://twitter.com/BBCAlLamont/status/918486378803089408

[9] https://twitter.com/BBCAlLamont/status/918488626744496129

[10] ibid

[11]https://thecelticblog.com/2017/10/blogs/the-takeover-panel-tells-the-court-that-king-is-not-an-unwitting-innocent/

[12]https://philmacgiollabhain.ie/2017/10/13/impecuniosity-and-credulity/#more-10337

[13]https://www.thescottishsun.co.uk/sport/football/1809658/rangers-agm-date-time-held-dave-king-mark-allen-attend/

[14]https://www.dailyrecord.co.uk/sport/football/football-news/five-key-points-rangers-agm-11614093

[15] ibid

[16] http://club1872.co.uk/wp-content/uploads/2017/12/AGM-2017-QA.pdf

[17]http://forum.rangersmedia.co.uk/topic/40673-is-celtics-allocation-at-ibrox-for-the-old-firm-match-fair/

[18]https://www.thescottishsun.co.uk/sport/football/1910671/rangers-fans-chief-agm-celtic-allocation-ibrox/

[19]https://www.dailyrecord.co.uk/sport/football/football-news/five-key-points-rangers-agm-11614093

[20]https://www.scotsman.com/sport/football/teams/rangers/dave-king-receives-bizarre-school-query-at-rangers-agm-1-4627922

[21] www.bbc.co.uk/sport/football/42454416

[22]www.eveningtimes.co.uk/sport/15790278.Court_of_Session_verdict_against_Dave_King_will_have_no_impact_on_Rangers__says_Ibrox_MD_Stewart_Robertson/

[23]www.heraldscotland.com/news/13063716.Revealed__how_Rangers_newco_was_shunned_by_major_banks/

[24] https://en.wikipedia.org/wiki/Metro_Bank_(United_Kingdom)

[25] www.bbc.co.uk/sport/football/42469305

[26] www.bbc.co.uk/news/uk-scotland-glasgow-west-43231582
[27] https://paddyontherailway.wordpress.com/2018/03/01/let-it-snow/
[28] ibid
[29] www.eveningtimes.co.uk/sport/rangers/15905423.Rangers_defender_Danny_Wilson_joins_MLS_side_ Colorado_Rapids/
[30] www.skysports.com/football/news/11788/11228915/rangers-confirm-interest-in-alfredo-morelos-from-chinese-club
[31] https://www.dailyrecord.co.uk/sport/football/football-news/rangers-reject-75m-alfredo-morelos-11941834
[32] www.hitc.com/en-gb/2018/01/31/report-beijing-renhe-offer-8million-for-rangers-striker-alfredo/
[33] https://www.thescottishsun.co.uk/sport/football/2237876/rangers-alfredo-morelos-fourth-bid-9million-beijing-renhe-south-american-clubs/
[34] https://www.thescottishsun.co.uk/sport/football/2276508/rangers-alfredo-morelos-beijing-renhe-nantes-emiliano-sala/
[35] www.talkingbaws.com/2018/02/bbc-reporter-claims-beijing-renhe-never-bid-alfredo-morelos-despite-8m-reports//
[36] https://www.thescottishsun.co.uk/sport/football/2173267/rangers-alfredo-morelos-bid-beijing-renhe-bbc-kheredine-idessane-tweet-sorry-apology/
[37] https://www.followfollow.com/forum/threads/kheredine-idessane-bbc-has-to-apologise-for-lying-about-morelos-bids.18180/
[38] https://videocelts.com/2018/02/blogs/latest-news/bbc-man-climbs-down/
[39] https://philmacgiollabhain.ie/2017/11/04/rugger-guy-analyses-rifc-2017-acccounts/#more-10450
[40] https://www.dailyrecord.co.uk/sport/football/football-news/rangers-chiefs-rubbish-cash-strapped-11987995
[41] ibid
[42] ibid
[43] https://philmacgiollabhain.ie/2018/02/17/rugger-guy-analyses-the-close-brothers-document/
[44] www.bbc.co.uk/news/uk-scotland-glasgow-west-43231582

Chapter 5

[1] https://www.bbc.co.uk/sport/football/42713345#tab-0/
[2] https://www.bbc.co.uk/sport/football/42763644
[3] ibid
[4] https://www.bbc.co.uk/sport/football/42713345#tab-0/
[5] https://www.dailyrecord.co.uk/sport/football/football-news/rangers-flop-

carlos-pena-booed-12006810

[6] https://www.bbc.co.uk/sport/football/42679262

[7]https://www.dailyrecord.co.uk/sport/football/football-match-reports/rangers-1-hibs-2-late-11964700

[8] https://www.bbc.co.uk/sport/football/43122595

[9] www.celticfc.net/news/14038

[10]https://www.dailyrecord.co.uk/sport/football/football-news/ugo-ehiogu-winner-rangers-made-12146370

[11]https://www.dailyrecord.co.uk/sport/football/football-news/whatever-happened-rangers-superleague-formula-12064739

[12] ibid

[13] ibid

[14] ibid

[15] https://www.bbc.co.uk/sport/football/43186420

[16]https://www.dailyrecord.co.uk/sport/football/football-news/graeme-murty-can-silence-rangers-12121444

[17] https://www.dailyrecord.co.uk/sport/football/football-news/rangers-can-give-celtic-fright-12110921

[18]https://www.dailyrecord.co.uk/sport/football/football-news/rangers-beat-celtic-sunday-because-12136058

[19]https://www.dailyrecord.co.uk/sport/football/football-news/celtic-boss-brendan-rodgers-worried-12123888

[20] http://forum.rangersmedia.co.uk/topic/314371-official-rangers-v-tarriers-thread/

[21]http://http://forum.rangersmedia.co.uk/topic/314371-official-rangers-v-tarriers-thread/?page=3

[22] https://www.dailyrecord.co.uk/sport/football/football-news/rangers-fans-campaign-blue-lines-12114327

[23]https://thecelticblog.com/2018/03/blogs/sevcos-sanctioned-fan-group-has-crossed-a-red-line-civic-scotland-cannot-just-ignore/

[24] ibid

[25] https://www.followfollow.com/forum/threads/cops-launch-probe-union-bears.22082/page-2

[26]https://www.dailyrecord.co.uk/sport/football/football-news/celtic-skipper-scott-brown-poster-12165249

[27] https://www.thescottishsun.co.uk/news/2345849/rangers-celtic-old-firm-ultra-union-bears-march/

[28]https://www.dailyrecord.co.uk/news/scottish-news/rangers-ultras-donned-balaclavas-masks-12167889

[29]www.eveningtimes.co.uk/sport/16067764.Willie_Collum_named_as_refer

ee_for_Rangers_v_Celtic_clash_at_ Ibrox/

[30] https://www.bbc.co.uk/sport/football/43275522

[31] ibid

[32] https://www.bbc.co.uk/sport/football/43365256

[33] https://www.thescottishsun.co.uk/sport/football/2346063/rangers-celtic-seven-things-we-learned-old-firm/

[34] ibid

[35] https://videocelts.com/2018/03/blogs/mcclair-hits-out-at-men-in-black/

[36] www.eveningtimes.co.uk/news/16140811.Scotland_striker_Leigh_Griffiths_defends_his_Irish_tricolour_celebrations_at_Ibrox_after_Celtic_win_over_Rangers/

[37] https://www.followfollow.com/forum/threads/a-scottish-internationalist-waving-an-irish-tricolour-worthy-of-debate.22595/

[38] ibid

[39] ibid

[40] www.talkingbaws.com/2018/03/leigh-griffiths-posts-hilarious-st-patricks-day-meme-week-flying-irish-flag/

[41] ibid

[42] https://www.followfollow.com/forum/threads/rtv-commentators.18864/

[43] https://celtsarehere.com/whats-the-goalie-doing-the-rangers-tv-commentary-is-must-see/ (Around the 44 second mark.)

[44] https://www.dailyrecord.co.uk/sport/football/football-match-reports/rangers-0-kilmarnock-1-kris-12205179

[45] https://www.theguardian.com/football/2018/mar/17/rangers-kilmarnock-scottish-premiership-match-report

[46] https://www.followfollow.com/forum/threads/silent-blessing-yet-again.23172/

[47] https://www.theguardian.com/football/2018/mar/17/rangers-kilmarnock-scottish-premiership-match-report (Comments section)

Chapter 6

[1] https://rangers.co.uk/news/headlines/season-ticket-renewal/

[2] www.vanguardbears.co.uk/article.php?i=165&a=fight-fire-with-fire

[3] ibid

[4] ibid

[5] http://forum.rangers-mad.co.uk/showthread.php?707127-The-World-s-Shame-(Updated)&highlight=thw+rold%27s+shame+mehmet

[6] ibid

[7] https://www.followfollow.com/forum/threads/the-worlds-shame.24334/

[8] ibid
[9] https://twitter.com/watp13/status/962740264656887809
[10] ibid
[11] https://twitter.com/FirstInGlasgow
[12] https://www.followfollow.com/forum/threads/masonic-snow.21060/
[13] ibid
[14] ibid
[15] https://twitter.com/KerryFail
[16] https://twitter.com/rico1872/status/968782686440558592
[17] https://www.followfollow.com/forum/threads/masonic-snow.21060/
[18] https://twitter.com/KTH_1989/status/968870271741562880
[19] www.vanguardbears.co.uk/article.php?i=166&a=remove-the-cancer
[20] https://twitter.com/pzj_1564/status/967876560215830528
[21] https://scotbritish.weebly.com/blog/welcome-to-the-crumbledome
[22]https://www.followfollow.com/forum/threads/safety-concerns-over-the-piggery-raised-with-hse.27313/
[23] https://twitter.com/pzj_1564/status/988768572632690688
[24]http://charity.celticfc.net/index
[25] https://twitter.com/pzj_1564/status/988833755761643520
[26] www.bbc.co.uk/news/uk-scotland-glasgow-west-23587678
[27] https://twitter.com/euan_meechan/status/902904407154675712
[28] https://twitter.com/pzj_1564/status/990680698833993729
[29] https://www.followfollow.com/forum/threads/the-worlds-shame.24334/
[30] https://twitter.com/DUPleader/status/858258655237615616
[31] www.vanguardbears.co.uk/about/
[32] ibid
[33] http://imperialbears.co.uk/
[34]http://imperialbears.co.uk/2017/09/04/another-sunday-and-another-attack-on-the-protestant-community/
[35] ibid
[36] ibid
[37] http://imperialbears.co.uk/
[38] http://imperialbears.co.uk/2017/06/11/215/
[39]http://forum.rangersmedia.co.uk/topic/310661-why-are-our-youth-teams-filled-with-tarriers/
[40] ibid
[41] www.bbc.co.uk/news/uk-43782241
[42]https://www.scotsman.com/news/opinion/dani-garavelli-powell-speech-renews-lifeblood-of-racist-uk-1-4724096 Comments section.
[43] http://imperialbears.co.uk/

167

[44] https://twitter.com/stwitty7/status/985435810110504966
[45] https://news.sky.com/story/football-association-launches-inquiry-into-child-sex-abuse-10674312
[46] www.bbc.co.uk/news/uk-scotland-38308254
[47] www.bbc.co.uk/news/uk-scotland-39553258
[48] https://www.thescottishsun.co.uk/news/scottish-news/259020/rangers-fired-abuse-quiz-coach-gordon-neely-after-boy-made-allegations-against-him/
[49] www.bbc.co.uk/news/uk-scotland-39553258
[50] http://forum.rangersmedia.co.uk/topic/306201-new-allegations-at-peado-fc-on-bbc-scotland/?page=13
[51] https://www.thescottishsun.co.uk/news/scottish-news/259020/rangers-fired-abuse-quiz-coach-gordon-neely-after-boy-made-allegations-against-him/
[52] www.bbc.co.uk/news/uk-scotland-39553258
[53] ibid
[54] https://twitter.com/RhebelRhebel/status/406403589062410240   (20 mins in)
[55] http://forum.rangersmedia.co.uk/topic/306201-new-allegations-at-peado-fc-on-bbc-scotland/?page=13
[56] http://forum.rangersmedia.co.uk/topic/306201-new-allegations-at-peado-fc-on-bbc-scotland/?page=12
[57] www.bbc.co.uk/news/uk-scotland-glasgow-west-44126217
[58] http://forum.rangersmedia.co.uk/topic/315917-bbc-article/
[59] ibid
[60] https://twitter.com/Swedleypops/status/996726282422554624
[61] http://forum.rangersmedia.co.uk/topic/315917-bbc-article/
[62] http://http://forum.rangersmedia.co.uk/topic/315917-bbc-article/?page=2
[63] ibid
[64] http://forum.rangersmedia.co.uk/topic/316099-sfa-bigot-exposed/?page=4
[65] http://forum.rangersmedia.co.uk/topic/306201-new-allegations-at-peado-fc-on-bbc-scotland/?page=12

Chapter 7

[1] https://www.thescottishsun.co.uk/sport/football/2313585/rangers-graeme-murty-celtic-scottish-cup/
[2] https://www.dailyrecord.co.uk/sport/football/football-news/celtic-boss-brendan-rodgers-no-12196511

[3]https://www.dailyrecord.co.uk/sport/football/football-news/no-offence-brendan-celtic-were-12352592

[4] https://www.bbc.co.uk/sport/football/43602413

[5] I definitely read this kind of reasoning on a Neo-Gers forum. Unfortunately, I forgot to save it and now can't find it!

[6]https://www.dailyrecord.co.uk/sport/football/football-news/rangers-striker-alfredo-morelos-promises-12281947

[7] https://www.dailyrecord.co.uk/sport/football/football-news/rangers-cant-spooked-scott-brown-12329003

[8]https://www.dailyrecord.co.uk/sport/football/football-news/fans-react-rangers-chairman-dave-12331094

[9] www.heraldscotland.com/news/16144564.rangers-4-dundee-0-score-tells-a-half-truth-as-rangers-win-ugly/?ref=mr&lp=16

[10]https://www.dailyrecord.co.uk/sport/football/football-news/celtic-vs-rangers-live-score-11767912

[11]https://www.thescottishsun.co.uk/sport/football/2286144/graeme-murty-bruno-alves-rangers-recall-earn/

[12]https://www.dailyrecord.co.uk/sport/football/football-transfer-news/rangers-refusal-bow-david-bates-12352668

[13] ibid

[14] https://playerswiki.com/bruno-alves

[15]https://philmacgiollabhain.ie/2017/07/20/one-big-unhappy-family/#more-9971

[16]https://www.dailyrecord.co.uk/sport/football/football-news/graeme-murty-tells-rangers-rebel-12360064

[17] https://www.bbc.co.uk/sport/football/43609086

[18] https://www.bbc.co.uk/sport/football/43705226

[19]https://www.scotsman.com/sport/tom-english-looks-back-at-the-1980-scottish-cup-final-riot-between-rangers-and-celtic-fans-and-asks-who-was-to-blame-1-1367411

[20]https://www.dailyrecord.co.uk/sport/football/football-news/brendan-rodgers-insists-celtic-rangers-12327052

[21]https://www.dailyrecord.co.uk/sport/football/football-news/brendan-rodgers-should-realise-celtics-12331400

[22]https://www.sundaypost.com/fp/scottish-premiership-post-split-fixtures-released-by-spfl/

[23]https://www.dailyrecord.co.uk/sport/football/football-news/graeme-murty-challenges-rangers-stars-12362906

[24]https://www.dailyrecord.co.uk/sport/football/football-news/celtic-boss-brendan-rodgers-reveals-12364209

[25] https://www.bbc.co.uk/sport/football/43686496
[26] https://www.dailyrecord.co.uk/sport/football/football-news/raging-andy-halliday-screams-rangers-12368370
[27] https://www.bbc.co.uk/sport/football/39249941
[28] https://www.dailyrecord.co.uk/sport/football/football-news/rangers-star-kenny-millers-wife-12369442
[29] https://www.dailyrecord.co.uk/sport/football/rangers-duo-alfredo-morelos-greg-12370548
[30] https://www.dailyrecord.co.uk/sport/football/football-news/inside-rangers-meltdown-details-emerge-12381975
[31] ibid
[32] ibid
[33] https://www.dailyrecord.co.uk/sport/football/football-news/good-riddance-kenny-miller-lee-12384677
[34] https://www.dailyrecord.co.uk/sport/football/football-news/rangers-chairman-dave-king-must-12375021 and
    https://www.dailyrecord.co.uk/sport/football/football-news/kenny-miller-rangers-great-hes-12381861
[35] https://www.dailyrecord.co.uk/sport/football/football-news/blundering-rangers-chief-dave-king-12381558.amp?__twitter_impression=true
[36] ibid
[37] https://www.dailyrecord.co.uk/sport/football/football-news/kenny-miller-lee-wallace-not-12380434
[38] https://www.dailyrecord.co.uk/sport/football/football-news/id-astonished-rangers-rebels-kenny-12386520
[39] https://www.dailyrecord.co.uk/sport/football/football-news/sacking-kenny-miller-would-rangers-12380636
[40] https://www.dailyrecord.co.uk/sport/football/football-news/mounting-unrest-rangers-squad-team-12387828.amp?__twitter_impression=true
[41] https://www.youtube.com/watch?v=lvhqU4smzN4
[42] https://www.thescottishsun.co.uk/sport/football/2540274/rangers-graeme-murty-daniel-candeias-andy-halliday/
[43] https://www.dailyrecord.co.uk/sport/football/football-news/mounting-unrest-rangers-squad-team-12387828.amp?__twitter_impression=true

Chapter 8

[1] https://twitter.com/Glesga7Giuseppe/status/928403592083656704
[2] https://twitter.com/jduffin24/status/963596782277152768
[3] https://twitter.com/jduffin24/status/965656741328445440

4 https://twitter.com/6inaRowHereWeGo/status/978646238739517440
5 ibid
6www.heraldscotland.com/news/16144683.Rangers_supporters_slammed_over_alleged__sectarian__singing_ and_assault/
7www.ibroxnoise.co.uk/2018/04/the-10-part-plan-to-rebuilding-rangers.html#more
8 https://rangers.co.uk/news/club/rangers-and-vaporized-partnership/
9 ibid
10 https://www.bhf.org.uk/heart-matters-magazine/news/e-cigarettes
11 ibid
12 https://ecigsuk.org.uk/take-vaping-dont-smoke/
13https://www.followfollow.com/forum/threads/rangers-announce-partnership-with-vapourised.24326/
14 ibid
15 ibid
16https://www.vaporized.co.uk/vaporized-rangers-name-the-flavour-competition-winners-announced/
17 ibid
18https://www.thescottishsun.co.uk/news/scottish-news/2662626/rangers-vape-flavours-names/
19https://www.scotsman.com/sport/football/competitions/premiership/rangers-anger-fans-with-green-boots-tweet-1-4717127
20https://philmacgiollabhain.ie/2018/04/04/the-colour-of-funny/#more-11205
21https://www.dailyrecord.co.uk/sport/football/football-news/rangers-confirm-hummel-kit-deal-12398402
22 https://hummel.co.uk/about-hummel/sponsorships-football
23 ibid
24https://www.dailyrecord.co.uk/sport/football/football-news/rangers-confirm-hummel-kit-deal-12398402
25https://www.rangersmegastore.com/CustomerServices/ContactUs/ContactForm
26 https://www.bbc.co.uk/sport/football/40358177
27https://www.followfollow.com/forum/threads/new-kit-retailer-dont-laugh.17770/
28https://www.thescottishsun.co.uk/sport/football/2654416/rangers-new-kit-strip-release-date-hummel/
29 http://forum.rangersmedia.co.uk/topic/315926-new-kit-delay/
30 ibid
31https://www.thescottishsun.co.uk/sport/football/2654416/rangers-new-

kit-strip-release-date-hummel/

[32]https://daviesleftpeg.wordpress.com/2018/04/25/tales-of-spiverythe-brown-brown-brogues-of-ibrox/

[33] http://forum.rangersmedia.co.uk/topic/315926-new-kit-delay/?page=2

[34] http://forum.rangersmedia.co.uk/topic/315926-new-kit-delay/?page=4

[35] http://forum.rangersmedia.co.uk/topic/315926-new-kit-delay/?page=5

[36]https://www.dailyrecord.co.uk/news/scottish-news/new-orange-rangers-strip-goes-12586079

Chapter 9

[1] https://www.bbc.co.uk/sport/football/43762819

[2]https://www.dailyrecord.co.uk/opinion/sport/chris-sutton-jimmy-calderwood-never-5577790

[3] https://twitter.com/celtichoff/status/989515447006527489

[4]https://www.dailyrecord.co.uk/sport/football/football-news/brendan-rodgers-wanted-celtic-lose-12412372

[5] https://www.bbc.co.uk/sport/football/43762819

[6]https://www.dailyrecord.co.uk/sport/football/football-news/brendan-rodgers-wanted-celtic-lose-12412372

[7] http://forum.rangersmedia.co.uk/topic/315345-the-official-taigs-v-rangers-match-thread/?page =1

[8]http://forum.rangersmedia.co.uk/topic/315295-happy-92nd-birthday-maam

[9] ibid

[10] ibid

[11] ibid

[12]https://www.dailyrecord.co.uk/sport/football/football-match-reports/celtic-5-rangers-0-hoops-12448401

[13]https://www.dailyrecord.co.uk/sport/football/football-news/rangers-refuse-allow-graeme-murty-12448720

[14] https://rangers.co.uk/news/club/rangers-player-year-dinner-2018/

[15] http://pfascotland.co.uk/commercial/awards-dinner/

[16] https://rangers.co.uk/news/club/rangers-player-year-dinner-2018/

[17] https://www.dailyrecord.co.uk/sport/football/football-news/rangers-fans-blast-club-going-12451817

[18] http://forum.rangersmedia.co.uk/topic/315485-poty-awards-tonight/

[19]https://www.thescottishsun.co.uk/news/2514602/rangers-murray-park-protest-banner-auchenhowie-celtic/

[20] http://forum.rangersmedia.co.uk/topic/315204-union-bears-statement/

[21]https://www.msn.com/en-gb/sports/football/celtic-fans-taunt-rangers-supporters-with-you-deserve-nothing-banner/ar-AAwv5Jv

[22]www.eveningtimes.co.uk/news/16193162.Watch__Moment_Rangers_fans_storm_own_Player_of_the_Year_Awards_in_Glasgow_after_Celtic_victory/

[23]http://http://forum.rangersmedia.co.uk/topic/315485-poty-awards-tonight/?page=9

[24]https://www.thescottishsun.co.uk/news/2573267/rangers-poty-glasgow-double-tree-hilton-player-of-the-year-fans-storm-venue/

[25]https://www.thescottishsun.co.uk/sport/football/2573305/rangers-player-of-the-year-daniel-candeias/

[26]http://http://forum.rangersmedia.co.uk/topic/315485-poty-awards-tonight/?page=17

[27]https://www.dailyrecord.co.uk/news/scottish-news/police-scotland-very-disappointed-mikael-12449887

[28]https://www.dailyrecord.co.uk/sport/football/football-news/dave-king-rangers-cronies-should-12372769

[29] ibid

[30]www.eveningtimes.co.uk/sport/16171937.Alastair_Johnston__Rangers_are__ahead_of_the_curve__on_the_ road_to_recovery/

[31]https://www.dailyrecord.co.uk/sport/football/football-news/alastair-johnston-statement-proves-rangers-12395512

[32]http://forum.rangersmedia.co.uk/topic/315274-alastair-johnston-statement-proves-rangers-board-are-out-of-touch-and-simply-dont-care/

[33]https://www.dailyrecord.co.uk/sport/football/football-news/graeme-murty-should-quit-rangers-12455906

[34] ibid

[35]https://www.dailyrecord.co.uk/sport/football/football-news/graeme-murty-quits-rangers-jus-12458646

[36]www.insidefutbol.com/2018/05/01/rangers-release-statement-graeme-murty-sacked/374075/

[37]https://www.dailyrecord.co.uk/sport/football/football-news/blame-board-graeme-murty-reaction-12459040

[38] ibid

[39] ibid

[40] ibid

[41]https://www.dailyrecord.co.uk/sport/football/football-news/rangers-board-replaces-professionals-patsies-12460587

[42]https://daviesleftpeg.wordpress.com/2018/04/25/tales-of-spiverythe-brown-brown-brogues-of-ibrox/

[43] https://daviesleftpeg.wordpress.com/2018/04/30/racist-at-club-1872/

[44]https://www.followfollow.com/forum/threads/our-current-situation-a-not-so-brief-synopsis.27388/

Chapter 10

[1]www.talkingbaws.com/2018/04/odds-slashed-steven-gerrard-becoming-new-rangers-manager/

[2]www.talkingbaws.com/2018/04/dave-king-spotted-anfield-everybody-thinks-steven-gerrard-talks/

[3]https://www.dailyrecord.co.uk/sport/football/football-news/taking-rangers-job-could-finish-12440661

[4]https://www.dailyrecord.co.uk/sport/football/football-news/rangers-appoint-steven-gerrard-weve-12439055

[5] ibid

[6] ibid

[7]https://www.dailyrecord.co.uk/sport/football/football-news/steven-gerrard-confirmed-rangers-manager-12442419

[8]https://www.dailyrecord.co.uk/sport/football/football-news/john-barnes-tells-steven-gerrard-12467543

[9] https://twitter.com/LFC_LION/status/992415057031122944?s=19

[10] https://www.lastditchtackle.com/rangers-fans-belt-out-sectarian-song-to-welcome-gerrard/

[11]https://videocelts.com/2018/05/blogs/latest-news/awkward-when-steven-gerrard-met-james-bell/

[12] https://twitter.com/PhantomFGAU/status/989512450029641728

[13]https://www.dailyrecord.co.uk/sport/football/football-news/steven-gerrard-backed-transfer-kitty-12467157

[14]https://www.dailyrecord.co.uk/sport/football/football-news/steven-gerrard-assurances-dave-king-12493000

[15]https://www.dailyrecord.co.uk/sport/football/football-news/dave-king-qa-full-rangers-12497577

[16]https://paddyontherailway.wordpress.com/2018/05/05/tragedy-tomorrow-comedy-tonight/

[17]www.thefa.com/get-involved/coach/the-boot-room/issue-28/steven-gerrard_fa-coaching-courses_170817

[18]www.heraldscotland.com/news/16197753.Regulator_gets_court_orders_forcing_Dave_King_to_make___11m_Rangers_shares_bid_with_cleared_funds/

[19] https://rangers.co.uk/news/headlines/paul-murray-and-barry-scott/

[20]https://www.dailyrecord.co.uk/sport/football/football-news/dave-king-qa-

full-rangers-12497577
[21] ibid
[22]https://www.dailyrecord.co.uk/sport/football/football-news/rangers-wont-near-celtic-6m-12520577
[23]https://www.dailyrecord.co.uk/sport/football/football-news/rangers-legend-ian-durrant-expects-12513814
[24] ibid
[25] www.worldfootball.net/teams/rangers-fc/1986/2/
[26] https://www.bbc.co.uk/sport/football/44062149
[27]https://www.dailyrecord.co.uk/sport/football/football-transfer-news/rangers-flop-eduardo-herrera-set-12171747
[28]https://www.thescottishsun.co.uk/sport/football/2624447/josh-windass-rangers-cardiff-burnley-transfer/
[29]https://www.thescottishsun.co.uk/sport/football/2624489/rangers-flop-dalcio-bids-farewell-as-ibrox-summer-exodus-begins/
[30]https://www.dailyrecord.co.uk/sport/football/football-transfer-news/josh-windass-emerges-3m-target-12515875
[31]www.eveningtimes.co.uk/sport/16220597.Steven_Gerrard_doesn__39_t_need_to_make_massive_changes_at_Rangers_this_summer__says_Jimmy_Nicholl/
[32]https://www.dailyrecord.co.uk/sport/football/football-news/jimmy-nicholl-confirms-rangers-exit-12529847
[33]https://www.dailyrecord.co.uk/sport/football/football-news/rangers-target-martin-skrtel-profiled-12478151
[34]https://www.dailyrecord.co.uk/sport/football/football-news/rangers-target-john-mcginn-steven-12514283
[35] ibid
[36]www.dailymail.co.uk/sport/football/article-5698001/Fenerbahce-issue-hands-warning-Rangers-Steven-Gerrards-target-Martin-Skrtel.html
[37]www.skysports.com/football/news/11095/11367111/should-wayne-rooney-join-steven-gerrard-at-rangers-paul-merson-and-craig-bellamy-discuss
[38]https://www.thescottishsun.co.uk/sport/football/2598438/dominic-solanke-rangers-steven-gerrard-loan/
[39]https://www.dailyrecord.co.uk/sport/football/football-news/steven-gerrard-rangers-thats-celtics-12479414
[40] https://daviesleftpeg.wordpress.com/2018/05/07/awaken-the-giant/

Chapter 11

[1] https://www.dailyrecord.co.uk/news/scottish-news/terror-threat-fears-see-roads-11040652

[2] https://www.thescottishsun.co.uk/news/scottish-news/2365589/rangers-celtic-pay-police-games-ibrox-parkhead-500000/

[3] www.talkingbaws.com/2018/02/bbc-reporter-claims-beijing-renhe-never-bid-alfredo-morelos-despite-8m-reports/

[4] https://www.dailyrecord.co.uk/sport/football/football-news/rangers-confirm-alfredo-morelos-bid-11960177

[5] https://thecelticblog.com/2018/01/blogs/beyond-embarrassment-sky-sports-news-is-still-trying-to-sell-moussa-dembele/

[6] https://www.thesun.co.uk/sport/football/5715789/brendan-rodgers-tells-arsenal-he-is-man-get-back-champions-league/

[7] https://www.bbc.co.uk/sport/football/41774039

[8] https://www.dailyrecord.co.uk/sport/football/football-news/derek-mcinnes-next-rangers-manager-11442911

[9] https://www.dailyrecord.co.uk/sport/football/football-news/derek-mcinnes-quit-aberdeen-rangers-11646679

[10] ibid

[11] ibid

[12] www.dailymail.co.uk/sport/football/article-5516609/Steve-Clarke-great-fit-Rangers-Celtic.html

[13] www.hitc.com/en-gb/2018/04/16/rangers-fans-want-steve-clarke-to-replace-murty-at-ibrox-after-o/

[14] https://www.dailyrecord.co.uk/sport/football/football-transfer-news/steve-clarke-not-go-rangers-12239487

[15] https://www.dailyrecord.co.uk/sport/football/football-news/rangers-wait-steven-gerrard-after-12434221

[16] https://www.msn.com/en-gb/sports/premier-league/rangers-aren-e2-80-99t-big-enough-for-nike-claims-football-kit-consultant/ar-AAweCa2

[17] ibid

[18] http://http://forum.rangersmedia.co.uk/topic/315213-hummel/?page=53&tab=comments

[19] https://www.dailyrecord.co.uk/sport/football/football-news/rangers-arent-big-enough-nike-12412853

[20] https://www.dailyrecord.co.uk/sport/football/football-news/celtics-big-guns-leave-rangers-12421262

[21] https://www.dailyrecord.co.uk/sport/football/football-news/steven-gerrard-appointment-excites-makes-12485027

[22] https://videocelts.com/2018/05/blogs/latest-news/rodgers-on-his-three-

day-break/

[23]https://www.telegraph.co.uk/sport/football/teams/liverpool/10730641/Liverpool-manager-Brendan-Rodgers-says-fear-of-failure-drives-him-on-in-chase-for-Premier-League-title.html

[24]https://www.dailyrecord.co.uk/sport/football/football-news/celtic-boss-brendan-rodgers-reveals-12364209

[25]https://www.dailyrecord.co.uk/sport/football/football-news/steven-gerrard-appointment-put-celtic-12519819

[26] ibid

[27]https://www.dailyrecord.co.uk/sport/football/football-news/steven-gerrard-should-miles-away-12432523

[28]https://www.dailyrecord.co.uk/sport/football/football-news/celtic-star-patrick-roberts-shown-11101590

[29] ibid

[30]https://www.dailyrecord.co.uk/sport/football/football-news/stars-flock-rangers-play-steven-12537201

[31] https://www.footballwhispers.com/players/scott-arfield

[32]https://theceltic blog.com/2018/05/blogs/shay-logan-an-arrogant-little-nobody-forever-trying-to-be-a-somebody/

[33]https://www.scotsman.com/sport/football/competitions/premiership/watch-shay-logan-sent-off-after-gesturing-towards-celtic-fans-1-4738864

[34]https://www.scotsman.com/sport/football/teams/hibernian/sending-off-was-worth-it-says-hibs-neil-lennon-1-4738990

[35] https://www.dailyrecord.co.uk/sport/football/football-news/rangers-fans-were-signing-sectarian-12529379

[36]https://www.dailyrecord.co.uk/sport/football/football-news/sectarianism-hibs-v-rangers-could-12534926

[37] https://twitter.com/tedermeatballs/status/995785374709485570

[38] https://www.youtube.com/watch?v=N16MkBZPW90

Chapter 12

[1] https://www.bbc.co.uk/sport/football/43854076

[2] https://www.bbc.co.uk/sport/football/43931906

[3] https://www.bbc.co.uk/sport/football/43931901

[4] https://www.bbc.co.uk/sport/football/43958074

[5] https://www.bbc.co.uk/sport/football/43939002

[6]https://www.dailyrecord.co.uk/sport/football/football-match-reports/hearts-1-celtic-3-moussa-12490345

[7]https://www.dailyrecord.co.uk/sport/football/football-news/hearts-cut-

grass-ahead-hibs-12507963

[8]https://www.dailyrecord.co.uk/sport/football/football-match-reports/hearts-2-hibs-1-steven-12507188

[9]https://www.dailyrecord.co.uk/sport/football/football-news/celtic-aberdeen-win-weekend-way-12506046

[10] ibid

[11] ibid

[12]https://www.dailyrecord.co.uk/sport/football/football-news/celtic-loan-model-full-flaws-12526813

[13]https://www.dailyrecord.co.uk/sport/football/football-match-reports/hibs-5-rangers-5-jamie-12526903

[14] https://www.bbc.co.uk/sport/football/44020123

[15]https://www.dailyrecord.co.uk/sport/football/football-news/cheats-fans-clash-over-celtic-12534240

[16] ibid

[17] ibid

[18] https://www.bbc.co.uk/sport/football/44020123

[19]http://forum.rangersmedia.co.uk/topic/315755-official-hibs-vs-rangers-match-thread/?page=95

[20] https://www.youtube.com/watch?v=-tjHlFPTwVk

[21] https://www.bbc.co.uk/sport/football/44145881

[22]https://www.dailyrecord.co.uk/sport/football/football-news/scotland-keeper-allan-mcgregor-suffers-8398094

[23] https://www.bbc.co.uk/sport/football/38658707

[24]https://www.lcfc.com/news/439614/leicester-city-sign-goalkeeper-eldin-jakupovi/featured

[25] https://www.bbc.co.uk/sport/football/40607449

[26]https://www.hullcitytigers.com/news/articles/2018/1718-player-of-the-year-awards-evening-round-up/

[27] https://www.bbc.co.uk/sport/football/championship/table

[28]https://www.hulldailymail.co.uk/sport/football/football-news/allan-mcgregor-wants-extend-hull-1252405

[29]www.dailymail.co.uk/sport/football/article-2591570/Allan-McGregor-ruled-rest-season-kidney-injury.html

[30]https://www.dailyrecord.co.uk/sport/football/football-news/scotland-keeper-allan-mcgregor-suffers-8398094

[31]https://www.dailyrecord.co.uk/sport/football/football-news/rangers-boss-steven-gerrard-details-12547215

[32] https://en.wikipedia.org/wiki/2017–18_Burnley_F.C._season

[33] https://www.footballwhispers.com/players/scott-arfield

[34]https://www.sportsmole.co.uk/football/burnley/transfer-talk/news/arfield-marney-to-leave-burnley_324454.html
[35]https://www.dailyrecord.co.uk/sport/football/football-news/stars-flock-rangers-play-steven-12537201
[36] ibid
[37]https://www.dailyrecord.co.uk/sport/football/football-news/money-wont-tempt-jermain-defoe-12553417
[38]https://www.followfollow.com/forum/threads/scottish-football-at-all-time-low.31076/
[39]https://www.dailyrecord.co.uk/sport/football/football-news/celtic-star-patrick-roberts-shown-11101590
[40]https://www.thescottishsun.co.uk/sport/football/2663346/celtic-kieran-tierney-rangers-kris-boyd/
[41] ibid
[42]https://www.thescottishsun.co.uk/sport/football/2652433/rangers-jermain-defoe-lucas-leiva-martin-skrtel-steven-gerrard/
[43]https://www.dailyrecord.co.uk/sport/football/football-news/money-wont-tempt-jermain-defoe-12553417
[44]https://www.thescottishsun.co.uk/sport/football/2652433/rangers-jermain-defoe-lucas-leiva-martin-skrtel-steven-gerrard/
[45]https://www.thescottishsun.co.uk/sport/football/2663256/rangers-kyle-bartley-steven-gerrard/
[46]https://www.yorkshireeveningpost.co.uk/sport/football/leeds-united/leeds-united-target-kyle-bartley-suffers-knee-injury-1-9142197
[47]https://www.thescottishsun.co.uk/sport/football/2651359/connor-goldson-rangers-brighton-bid-rejected-reports-steven-gerrard-ibrox/

Chapter 13

[1]https://www.dailyrecord.co.uk/sport/football/football-news/veteran-rangers-defender-bruno-alves-12553896
[2]https://www.footballinsider247.com/rangers-have-no-choice-but-to-offload-key-first-teamer-after-dave-king-investment-revelation/
[3]http://www.ibroxnoise.co.uk/2018/05/two-confirmed-departures-two-pending.html
[4]https://www.dailyrecord.co.uk/sport/football/alfredo-morelos-linked-rangers-exit-12561432
[5]https://www.dailyrecord.co.uk/sport/football/football-news/rangers-fans-react-over-claim-12566543
[6]https://www.dailyrecord.co.uk/sport/football/football-news/michael-

ohalloran-sorry-rangers-striker-12568191

[7] https://www.footballinsider247.com/excuses-from-rangers-ace-are-absolutely-laughable-from-a-player-taking-gers-for-mugs/

[8] https://www.dailyrecord.co.uk/news/scottish-news/rangers-striker-michael-ohalloran-targeted-12544705

[9] ibid

[10] ibid

[11] https://www.dailyrecord.co.uk/sport/football/football-news/michael-ohalloran-sorry-rangers-striker-12568191

[12] http://www.ibroxnoise.co.uk/2018/05/major-rangers-target-formally-rejects.html

[13] http://www.hitc.com/en-gb/2018/05/21/do-has-lazios-lucas-leiva-just-killed-rangers-dreams-of-summer-t/

[14] https://www.dailyrecord.co.uk/sport/football/football-transfer-news/martin-skrtel-posts-cryptic-social-12579834

[15] https://www.lastditchtackle.com/paddy-power-steven-gerrard-evens-to-be-sacked-before-end-of-next-season/

[16] https://www.bettingpro.com/category/football/william-hill-steven-gerrard-rangers-betting-odds-specials-20180505-0007/

[17] https://www.dailyrecord.co.uk/sport/football/football-news/rangers-under-steven-gerrard-good-12577052

[18] https://www.dailyrecord.co.uk/sport/football/football-news/steven-gerrard-rangers-thats-not-12568570

[19] https://www.dailyrecord.co.uk/sport/football/football-news/theres-conspiracy-against-rangers--12544952

[20] http://etims.net/?p=8796

[21] https://www.thescottishsun.co.uk/sport/football/1532482/sfa-compliance-officer-investigation-rangers-uefa-licence-2011-stewart-regan/

[22] https://www.dailyrecord.co.uk/sport/football/football-news/rangers-charged-sfa-over-2011-12540555

[23] https://rangers.co.uk/news/headlines/notice-of-complaint/

[24] https://www.dailyrecord.co.uk/sport/football/football-news/sfa-grant-rangers-uefa-licence-12512478

[25] https://www.bbc.co.uk/sport/football/44218554

[26] https://www.dailyrecord.co.uk/sport/football/football-news/sfa-director-who-ruled-rangers-12586575

[27] http://forum.rangersmedia.co.uk/topic/316099-sfa-bigot-exposed/?page=2

[28] https://www.followfollow.com/forum/threads/sfa-board-member-gary-hughes-probed-after-labelling-rangers-fans-"the-great-unwashed".31512/

29 ibid
30 ibid
31 http://forum.rangersmedia.co.uk/topic/316099-sfa-bigot-exposed/
32http://forum.rangersmedia.co.uk/topic/316099-sfa-bigot-exposed/?page=2
33https://thecelticblog.com/2017/09/blogs/the-evidence-of-sfa-collusion-over-ebts-is-piling-up-its-another-day-of-shame-for-the-hacks/
34 http://www.dailymail.co.uk/sport/football/article-2116686/Rangers-crisis-Campbell-Ogilvie-received-95k-EBT-cash.html
35https://www.dailyrecord.co.uk/sport/football/football-news/sfa-director-who-ruled-rangers-12586575
36https://www.dailyrecord.co.uk/sport/football/football-news/rangers-chief-dave-king-calls-12589512
37 https://rangers.co.uk/news/headlines/season-tickets-a-thank-you/
38https://www.dailyrecord.co.uk/sport/football/football-news/rangers-decision-cut-celtics-ticket-12597588
39 https://www.dailyrecord.co.uk/sport/football/football-news/rangers-only-cutting-celtics-allocation-12600028
40 http://forum.rangersmedia.co.uk/topic/316106-beggars-allocation-cut/
41 ibid
42 ibid
43 https://twitter.com/RangersObserver/status/999624888045457408
44http://www.eveningtimes.co.uk/sport/rangers/16242883.Martin_Skrtel_won_t_be_joining_former_Liverpool_team-mate_Steven_Gerrard_at_Rangers/
45https://www.dailyrecord.co.uk/sport/football/football-transfer-news/rangers-want-martin-skrtel-insists-12581421

Chapter 14

1https://www.gersnet.co.uk/index.php/online-museum/history-articles/489-the-rangers-trophy-room
2 https://philmacgiollabhain.ie/2018/05/27/schadenfreude-and-pre-orders/
3https://www.dailyrecord.co.uk/news/business-consumer/tubes-orange-smarties-back-spring-12522760
4https://philmacgiollabhain.ie/2018/05/27/the-desire-for-democracy-in-the-blue-room/
5https://www.dailyrecord.co.uk/news/scottish-news/former-rangers-stars-face-24m-12607046
6https://www.thescottishsun.co.uk/news/scottish-news/1329654/rangers-

barry-ferguson-transfer-mansion-wife-bankruptcy/

[7] https://twitter.com/RogueRFCStaffer/status/1001091644593229825

[8] https://www.dailyrecord.co.uk/news/scottish-news/rangers-management-duo-steven-gerrard-12603532

[9]http://www.eveningtimes.co.uk/news/16248827.Celtic_release_statement_about_Parkhead_ticket_ allocations_after_Rangers_cut/

[10] https://www.dailyrecord.co.uk/sport/football/football-news/rangers-only-cutting-celtics-allocation-12600028

[11]https://www.dailyrecord.co.uk/sport/football/football-news/rangers-right-cut-celtic-allocation-12591689

[12]https://www.dailyrecord.co.uk/sport/football/football-news/rangers-celtic-slashing-ticket-allocations-12610881

[13]https://www.dailyrecord.co.uk/sport/spfl-insist-murdoch-maclennans-links-12612812

[14]https://www.dailyrecord.co.uk/sport/football/football-news/rangers-chairman-dave-king-calls-12617067

[15] http://forum.rangersmedia.co.uk/topic/316170-spfl-chairman/

[16] ibid

[17] ibid

[18] Ibid

44139853R00115

Printed in Poland
by Amazon Fulfillment
Poland Sp. z o.o., Wrocław